# POETRY MENTOR TEXTS

# POETRY MENTOR TEXTS
## Making Reading and Writing Connections, K–8

Lynne R. Dorfman
Rose Cappelli

Foreword by Georgia Heard

Stenhouse
PUBLISHERS

Portland, Maine

Stenhouse Publishers
www.stenhouse.com

Library of Congress Cataloging-in-Publication Data
Dorfman, Lynne R., 1952-
  Poetry mentor texts : making reading and writing connections, K-8 / Lynne R. Dorfman and Rose Cappelli. -- 2nd ed.
      p. cm.
  Includes bibliographical references.
  ISBN 978-1-57110-949-1 (pbk. : alk. paper) -- ISBN 978-1-57110-972-9 (ebook)
  1.  Poetry--Study and teaching (Elementary) 2.  Poetry--Authorship--Study and teaching (Elementary) 3.  Poetry--Study and teaching (Middle School) 4.  Poetry--Authorship--Study and teaching (Middle school)  I. Cappelli, Rose, 1950- II. Title.
  LB1575.D67 2012
    372.64'044--dc23

                              2012022960

Chapter opener photos by Rose Cappelli and Jon DeMinico
Cover photo by Rose Cappelli
Cover design, interior design, and typesetting by designboy Creative Group

Manufactured in the United States of America

PRINTED ON 30% PCW
RECYCLED PAPER

18 17 16 15 14 13 12   9 8 7 6 5 4 3 2 1

# CREDITS

**Chapter 5**

**Chapter 6**

For our editor and friend, Bill Varner:

**E**ffective communicator,
**D**elivering efficient messages to
**I**nspire confidence and empower
**T**he diverse team
**O**f teacher-writers with the
**R**ight words at the right time.

# Contents

# foreword

by Georgia Heard

Lynne Dorfman and Rose Cappelli have done it again! They've given us a treasure chest of mentor texts—this time for poetry.

I've always believed, just as Lynne and Rose do, that there is more than one writing teacher in every classroom to guide student writers. In fact, a crowd of invisible teachers quietly whispers words of wisdom to students as they write. Mentor texts—the books and poems we love that can stretch writers to do their best—help students stay true to their vision of what they really want to say.

One of the challenges that teachers of reading and writing face is how to get these high-quality exemplar texts into the classroom to use in literature circles, small- and whole-group instruction, and mini-lessons, and to inspire our students to write their best. The poetry choices are abundant and sometimes overwhelming—not to mention that school budgets are tight. *Poetry Mentor Texts* is the perfect guide to help us on our journey of locating the just-right poem to inspire and guide our students in writing and reading poetry.

This book's predictable structure is very user friendly and encompasses both reading and writing connections. Each chapter is devoted to a particular student-friendly poetic form, such as the list poem, acrostic poem, and poem for two voices. Five excellent mentor poems have been carefully selected for each chapter to move student writers forward by highlighting several essential writing traits, such as word choice, point of view, and figurative language.

As I read *Poetry Mentor Texts*, I found poems by some of my favorite children's poets, including J. Patrick Lewis and Kristine O'Connell George, and also discovered new poets, such as Stenhouse's very own William Varner. In addition to these grown-up mentor poems, Lynne and Rose sprinkle each chapter with excellent student samples that will be sure to spark your own students' creative powers.

Every writer of poetry is first a reader of poetry. *Poetry Mentor Texts* will open a treasure chest of poems to inspire your students to raise the level of expectation for their own poems and write from their hearts.

# Acknowledgments

*You will find poetry nowhere unless you bring some of it with you.*

➢ *Joseph Joubert*

Mentors have always played an important role in our personal and professional lives. We continue to learn from the work of all the authors of children's literature. For this book particularly, we relied on the work of Joyce Sidman, Georgia Heard, Ralph Fletcher, J. Patrick Lewis, Sara Holbrook, and Kristine O'Connell George. Many teacher-writers have also influenced our thinking as we continue to grow as teachers of readers and writers— Katie Wood Ray, Regie Routman, Mark Overmeyer, Kelly Gallagher, Debbie Miller, and Jeff Anderson.

We are so grateful for our friendships with poet-teachers Bruce Bloome and Will Mowery. Thank you for providing us with wonderfully wonderful poems for this book. A special thank-you goes to Bill Varner, our poet-editor, for sharing his poetry with us. It inspired us to return to our notebooks and write.

The support of our friends and colleagues of the Keystone State Reading Association and our own Chester County Reading Association is never-ending. Thank you for always cheering us on! As ever, we appreciate the encouragement and advice from Patti and Phil Sollenberger and Denise Glick at Reading Matters, the Stenhouse distributor for our area.

Our work with the Pennsylvania Writing and Literature Project continues to be an important part of our professional growth. Thank you, Dr. Mary Buckelew, for the many opportunities you have afforded us. We are proud to be members of such a strong writing community. We learn from all the teachers we meet through our graduate courses, presentations, and conferences. The Project has provided us with much food for thought.

Our work in our districts, Upper Moreland Township School District and the West Chester Area School District, has been rewarding and empowering. We extend our thanks to our superintendents, Dr. Robert Milrod and Dr. Jim Scanlon, and our principals, Dr. Joseph M. Waters and Mrs. Rebecca Eberly. Of course, our work would not be possible without the help of the extraordinary teachers and students who provide inspiration and insight on a daily basis. We especially thank Teresa Lombardi, Mickey Moore, Joanne Costello, Jon De-Minico, Danielle Norton, Karen Drew, Bruce Bloome, and Sue Powdizki from Upper Moreland Intermediate School, and Linda Trembath, Connie Harker, Nicole Lockhart, Christine Miller, and Shawn Dzielawa from Fern Hill Elementary School.

Our friend, author Frank Murphy, has been a most enthusiastic supporter of our work. Thank you, Frank, for the incredible samples of persona poetry from your fifth graders at Holland Elementary School in the Council Rock School District. We would also like to thank Mr. Mark J. Klein, Esq., the superintendent of Council Rock School District, and Mr. Andrew Sanko, the principal of Holland Elementary School.

The Stenhouse crew continues to be our extended family. You warm our hearts and give us the stamina to continue to write books and share our work with teachers across the country. A big thank-you goes to Chandra Lowe, Jill Cooley, Rebecca Eaton, Chuck Lerch, Nate Butler, Chris Downey, Zsofia McMullin, Lise Wood, and Jay Kilburn. Of course, we would like to express our gratitude to Philippa Stratton and Dan Tobin for their tireless work to maintain Stenhouse Publishers as a cutting-edge educational publishing firm. And most especially, thank you, Bill Varner, our editor and friend. We could not have written any of our books without you. We have so much respect for you and your advice. You are most remarkable!

Thank you, Ralph and Allan, for always being there. Allan, we're still waiting for your chapter . . . .

# Introduction

Teaching kids of all ages to write poetry, and to love to write and read poetry,
is probably my favorite teaching. It's sheer fun. It's exhilarating.
Every child is successful. Each year, I am amazed at what kids can do,
how insightful and clever they are, and what powerful poems they write.

➤ *Regie Routman*, Conversations

Should everyone read and write poetry? You may think, "It's not for me. I don't get it, don't like it, and my students don't like it either." But kids *do* love poetry! They like the rhythm of the words, the rhyme, and the playful, often humorous tones. Kids love to sing and listen to music. Poetry is like music: it has lyrics, melody, and harmony. It's why we like to read poems aloud—a symphony of sounds emerges and engages our senses in a whirlwind of images, emotions, and wonderings about the world and how things work.

Poetry is the great equalizer for both reading and writing workshop. Using a poem as a mentor text for reading and writing is doable. A poem's length invites revisiting for different purposes. Its vivid language pulls the reader in and provides opportunities for word investigations. Poems make great reading selections for literature circles and small-group instruction, either read individually or compared as a set. They are effective for small- and whole-group instruction because they are short and can be reread many times to deepen comprehension, cite evidence, offer opinions, draw conclusions, and talk about main ideas and themes. In *Pass the Poetry, Please!* Lee Bennett Hopkins discusses how poems are effective reads for struggling readers in the upper grades:

> Poems, being short, are not demanding or frustrating to these readers. They can start them, finish them, and gain from them, without experiencing any discomfort whatsoever. (1987, 6)

Poetry shouldn't be just a part of the language arts curriculum. It offers another way to communicate and demonstrate our understanding of a concept in content areas. It is a method for deepening comprehension and developing a level of empathy and knowledge that can be applied to real-world situations. Poetry can serve to informally assess science and math. It can help students link content areas. As poet Sara Holbrook says:

> We write poetry to make our individual ideas heard, and these ideas must not be limited to language arts class . . . When we succeed, when we create a poem that serves as a bridge toward understanding, that is communication—an indispensable standard of learning. (2005, xvi)

## THE TOP TEN REASONS TO USE POETRY AS MENTOR TEXTS

We have many ideas about why poetry should be regularly used in reading/writing classrooms, but we tried to consolidate our thinking into a simple list. Here are our top ten reasons to use poetry as mentor texts:

1.  Children love the sound of language and the chance to read, recite, and perform poetry.
2.  Poetry can help us see differently, understand ourselves and others, and validate our passions and our human experience.
3.  Poetry easily finds a home in all areas of the curriculum and can bridge the reading/writing workshop.
4.  Poetry is the great equalizer—a genre especially suited to the struggling or unmotivated reader/writer.
5.  Poetry enhances thinking skills and promotes personal connections.
6.  Reading poems aloud captures the ear, imagination, and soul of the listener.
7.  The playfulness of language and the ability of words to hold us captive with their intensity, beauty, and genius are particularly apparent in poetry.
8.  A poet helps us see things in new ways and helps us talk and write about ordinary things in extraordinary ways. That's the essence of good writing.
9.  Poetry helps broaden children's experiences and what they are able to write about.
10. Poetry can be the voice that names the events we live through by helping us make sense of them and write about them.

## HOW TO NAVIGATE THIS BOOK

Our introduction provides you with a rationale for poetry use in reading and writing workshop. In Chapter 1 we define mentor texts and discuss the natural connections between reading and writing. This chapter also provides an explanation of possible ways to integrate poetry into a school day and a look at the power of companion pieces (books, other poems, songs). The rest of this book is organized into six chapters that deal with, respectively, poetry to inspire response, list poems, acrostic poetry, persona poetry, and poetry for two voices. The final chapter contains an annotated list of resources for the poems and companion pieces we discuss in each chapter as well as additional resources too good to miss. We hope to provide you with more than enough choices to last an entire year.

Additionally, each chapter includes classroom connections for both reading and writing. The poems we have highlighted focus on the five critical reading areas whenever possible: phonemic awareness, phonics, vocabulary, fluency, and comprehension. We believe that the use of poetry in all grades directly links to the charge of text complexity presented in today's Common Core State Standards. Poetry addresses the standards' emphasis on sophisticated text and the skills with which students read. It helps students deepen their comprehension by requiring them to respond to reading—orally and/or written—to draw inferences, and to determine the impact that point of view has on the text.

Each mentor poem also serves to move our student writers forward by presenting them with an opportunity for discussion of the traits of writing, such as the development of ideas (content), organization, voice, and conventions. You can choose which area(s) you wish to expand in a shared or guided experience, depending on what your student writers need. We don't discuss every pillar of reading and every trait of writing—instead, we focus on the ones that seem to naturally fit with the poem presented or the developmental level of the target audience.

Each chapter includes classroom snapshots from reading and writing workshop and presents five poems for your use. Student samples help you see what you might expect your own students to compose. Finally, Your Turn Lessons appear at the end of each chapter for you to try out for yourself and with your students. These lessons may be taught over two or three days. They are longer than the traditional mini-lesson because they focus on a strategy or skill that you want all your students to be able to try out and eventually use independently as readers and writers. The Your Turn Lesson scaffolds the gradual release of responsibility model and provides a place for reflection so that students' understanding of the target skill or strategy is deepened.

## Your Turn Lesson Format

| | |
|---|---|
| Hook: | Use literature to invite participation. |
| Purpose: | Tell what you will do. |
| Brainstorm: | Invite writers to sketch, list, talk, create word storms, etc., to generate ideas. |
| Model: | Demonstrate what you will do with a mentor text, your own writing, or sometimes a student sample. |
| Shared/Guided Writing: | Writers actively participate in the modeled technique or strategy, either individually, in partnerships, or as part of a whole-class shared writing experience. Use partner or group sharing and roving conferences to guide writers. |
| Independent Writing: | Writers compose a new piece or return to a published piece or notebook entry to try out the strategy. |
| Reflection: | Writers consciously reflect on how the writing worked. Reflection is an important step that helps students view themselves as writers and become aware of the strategies that work for them and that move them forward. Self-reflection can be guided through the use of key questions. All writers should first reflect on the strategy that was demonstrated and tried out. |

> ➢    How did today's strategy work?

Additional questions can be varied according to the level of the writer and the purpose of the lesson.

➢ What do I do well as a writer? What are the unique characteristics that set my writing apart from others (my fingerprints)?
➢ If I were to revise, what is one thing I would absolutely change, omit, or add?
➢ Would this piece of writing work better in a different format? A different tense?

*Optional Steps*

Write and Reflect Again:   Writers rewrite their entry or piece using the revision strategy from the reflection. Writers ask themselves if this is a piece they wish to continue to work on for publication.

Goal Setting:   Writers use input from the selection to set personal goals.

The Your Turn Lesson provides a chance for you to write along with your students. As a teacher of writers, it is important to be a teacher who writes. In *A Garden of Poets: Poetry Writing in the Elementary Classroom*, Mary Kenner Glover talks about the importance of teacher as writer:

The teacher must be a writer, too. I have been most successful as a poetry teacher when I've let my students know from the beginning that I am a writer also. When they write, I write alongside them. They see me filling the pages of my writer's notebook as they are beginning to fill theirs. I become their equal in this way, and although I maintain my role as their teacher and guide, I am just one writer among many. (1999, 21)

## FINAL THOUGHTS

The simple truth is that poetry—like art, music, and other forms of creativity—can develop a sense of compassion and empathy that children need to better understand themselves and their world. Beauty and humanity are inextricably woven together into poetic expression. As Donald Graves reminds us:

We are surrounded by poetry in the ordinary moments of our days. We can take the ordinary and, through poetry, turn the smallest, least significant moment into something important. In this respect, poetry is for everyone. (1994, 340)

The use of poetry as mentor texts in reading and writing will give students a chance to grow as readers, writers, imagineers, and human beings. That is where the power lies. Join us as we float on a sea of words to catch some views of reading and writing workshop where poems are used as mentor texts.

Happy reading!

# Getting Started

## Editing the Chrysalis
*by Avis Harley*

"**A**t last," cried Butterfly,

**P**oised
**O**ver its
**E**mpty chrysalis,
"**M**y final draft!"

# WHAT ARE MENTOR TEXTS?

We believe that the use of mentor texts is a powerful way to move students forward as writers. In our previous books, we have defined a mentor text as a piece of writing—a picture book, novel, magazine article, informational book, essay, or poem—that you can return to many times in the course of a year and for many reasons. By imitating mentor texts, young writers dare to take risks and try out new things and, as a result, stretch their skills and grow. Mentor texts provide multiple opportunities for scaffolding sentence structures, placement of words, the use of a particular craft or punctuation mark, and countless other aspects of good writing.

Mentor texts exist on many levels and often span levels. For example, in first grade, we could make personal connections with the topics of Jack Prelutsky's poems and use them as springboards for writing pieces. In second grade, we could take a poem such as Prelutsky's "My Sister Ate an Orange" as a way to talk about surprise endings or rhyme patterns. In third grade we can return to the poem to talk about the author's use of humor. Perhaps you want to show how writers often write about ordinary things but present them in original ways. In middle school you might use Pat Mora's "Legal Alien" to think about the compare/contrast format, the metaphors, and the effective repetition. In high school, students can read Mora's poem and read a companion poem such as "I, Too" by Langston Hughes to think about the voice established in both poems before finding their voice to write a personal essay or poem about what it is like to be torn between two worlds or simply to be a part of two worlds.

Students begin to find their own mentor texts as they fall in love with a book or an author. They begin to study what that author does to create a text—how it is organized, how punctuation is used, and how the content is developed. They notice the words an author chooses to carry his ideas, the sounds and rhythms of those words, the lengths of the sentences, and the imagery used to stir feelings in the reader and make him think and imagine. Then students choose what they need for a particular piece of writing and imitate the author in one or many ways.

The universal goal of learning is transfer. In *How People Learn* (Bransford, Brown, and Cocking 2001), the authors discuss how transfer involves learning with deep understanding, not just committing facts to memory. They talk about the importance of organizing information into a conceptual framework to teach it and then assessing what was studied for understanding. In writing classrooms, we want our students to take all that they have gathered from studying mentor authors and apply this new learning to their own writing. They learn how to make good decisions by trying out several possibilities and choosing what best works in the form, genre, and topic they are currently drafting. In this way they are reflecting on their literary practices and taking charge of their learning. The final assessment is the final draft or the draft's journey through multiple revisions. Here, teachers can see the tracks of their own teaching and the transfer of learning from the study of mentor texts and authors.

# MAKING READING-WRITING CONNECTIONS

The best way to get started using poetry in reading and writing workshop is to read all kinds of poems so that your students can figure out what it is they are able to imitate. Some students will love to read and write rhyming poetry and others will need to experience free-verse poems so they can imitate the rhythms and structures. Students may be surprised at the selection of titles in the poetry section of the school and public library and the connections they make to everyday life, to feelings about family and friends, and across content areas such as history, science, and math. Paul Janeczko (1999) reminds us: "While you are capturing your thoughts and experiences in your journal, don't forget that you cannot be a good writer—poet or prose writer—if you are not a reader" (10).

When you use mentor texts for the lessons and conference focus of your writing workshop, there are often natural connections to reading workshop. In *For the Good of the Earth and Sun: Teaching Poetry*, Georgia Heard (1989) reminds us, "Every writer of poetry is first a reader of poetry" (1). We believe that daily read-alouds using poetry will help students make reading-writing connections, improve vocabulary and fluency, and deepen comprehension. Poetry enhances thinking skills and enables students to make personal connections. There are many ways to build bridges between writing and reading workshop. For instance, when you are working on building content through showing rather than telling, it is a good time to teach or review the skill of inferring in your reading workshop.

When you are teaching your readers about visualization and how the writer paints pictures with words, you can talk about snapshots of characters, setting, and objects in writing workshop. As readers, the students start to understand their job as writers. They are like artists, using specific words to create the many tones and hues that color their readers' thinking and stir up intense feelings—passion! Students can begin to collect the rich descriptions of people and places in their reader response journals or writer's notebooks and use them to create poems about family members, pets, secret hiding places, favorite vacation spots, or the characters and imagined settings for new stories they will write.

In writing workshop, the student can revisit the poem with a partner or individually to try to imitate the structure, the use of a literary device such as simile, the rhythm, the rhyme scheme, or the tone. In one fifth-grade classroom, students were reading poems that centered on color, such as the collection of poems in *Hailstones and Halibut Bones* by Mary O'Neill, "February" by Charlotte Otten in *January Rides the Wind*, and poems in *Nature's Paintbox: A Seasonal Gallery of Art and Verse* by Patricia Thomas. Students were encouraged to examine poetry books in the classroom library, the school library, and public library. Some students brought favorites from home. They marked poems that used color in some way and chose one or two to share in whole group. Students were directed to turn and talk with a partner about their poem—how it made them feel and what they noticed about the way it was written. Some of these poems were read by a pair of students or a small group. Some students actually chose to perform their poems with gestures and movements. They were deeply immersed in the poems before they started to write one of their own. Michelle, a fifth grader, came across "Lullaby" by Eve Merriam in her own search for color poems. She closely imitated Eve Merriam's work in her poem "Valentine's Day."

Pink,
Pink,
Heart
Cards.

Pink as a puppy's nose
Pink as the polish on your toes.

Pink for the day
When Cupid appears.

Light and lovely,
Dazzling and dainty,
Show-your-love time.

Pink,
Pink.
Sharing cards
Caring cards.

Think
Pink
All day long.

# THE QUESTION POEM

The question poem is an easy way to get students to make reading-writing connections. Question poems will stimulate conversations and help students find common understandings as they wonder about things they've studied in and out of school. The question poem gives students an opportunity to reflect about their lives—looking inward and outward. Ralph Fletcher (1996) in *A Writer's Notebook* explores the writing of "fierce wonderings." He says this kind of writing forces you to pay attention to "what haunts you, what images or memories keep running around in your mind even when you try not to think about them" (16).

When we read question poems with students, we have a stimulating conversation. According to poet Sara Holbrook (2005), writing the question poem will help students find and remember what they want to know about instead of finding the answers to questions that their teachers may pose. Like scientists and artists, writers ask lots of questions, observe their world closely, and gather information from their observations. We structure our thinking into relationships such as compare and contrast, cause and effect, problem and solution. Sometimes the question poem is written in the writer's notebook and is purely a personal wondering of the writer. At other times, it may help teachers to introduce a unit of study, using the question poems students have written in their writer's notebook in place of K-W-L-S (Know-Want to Know-Learned-Still Wondering). At the end of the unit, students may return to their writer's notebook to write a new question poem. The question poem may be an individual or a collaborative effort. If students write collaboratively, it gives them a chance to synthesize and evaluate their learning before reaching consensus about a final draft. These new poems remind our students that, as lifelong learners, there should be new questions after we read and study new material.

Before or after a unit about environmental awareness or conservation you may decide to use "Will We Ever See?" by Georgia Heard as a mentor poem. Students can easily imitate her wonderings about animal extinction. Notice how the second line of each couplet starts with a strong verb.

### Will We Ever See?
#### by Georgia Heard

Will we ever see a tiger again,
stalking its prey with shining eyes?

Will we see the giant orangutan
inspecting its mate for fleas?

Or a California condor
feeding on the side of a hill?

Or a whooping crane
walking softly through a salty marsh?

Or hear the last of the blue whales
singing its sad song under the deep water?

Other possible mentor poems for questioning include "Crow" by Joyce Sidman and "What's the Point?" by Sara Holbrook.

# POETRY: WHEN AND WHERE

In his book *Learning Under the Influence of Language and Literature: Making the Most of Read-Alouds Across the Day*, Lester Laminack shares his vision for read-alouds in the classroom. He states, "Poetry is a powerful form of writing that can say big things in small spaces and give students more control over their choices as writers" (Laminack and Wadsworth 2006, 114). We believe that integrating poetry into our daily routines as a time for thinking and imagining the possibilities has great value. Just before lunch—or anytime during the day when it is possible to share a poem—is a great time to hook your students and make them hungry for more. Think about using the time while your class is lined up waiting for the art teacher or gym teacher. What about at the end of the day when they are sitting at their desks and waiting for the final bell? What about a poem displayed on chart paper or the board when the students enter the room as a way to respond in their reader response journal or to prompt writing in their writer's notebook? Teachers can use one poem for an entire week (or for just a day or two), and many times can use the same poem in both reading and writing workshop.

## One Possible Format to Get Started with Poetry in Your Classroom

There are many ways to incorporate poetry into the reading/writing classroom and across your day. We want you to enjoy poetry for its sights, sounds, smells, and all the emotions that it stirs up in your students and you. Poetry is meant to be read aloud; we hope students will find their favorite poems, read them often, and even copy them into their writer's notebook. Eventually these poems may spark an original poem or a flurry of poems that students can share during the composing process and after they are published.

Introduce poetry at the beginning of the year by collecting books from your school and local library as well as your own personal collection. Immerse students in the reading of poetry. It's a great idea to allow students to sit in their choice spot in the classroom and read with a partner or individually. Ask students to try to notice how poetry is different from other genres. What are they noticing about poetry? Students can share their noticings at the end of every writing workshop period for several days or even an entire week. Post this anchor chart in a poetry corner or on a writing workshop bulletin board. Allowing your student poets to add to this anchor chart and initial their entry as they make new discoveries instills a sense of ownership in their learning. You may want to have students copy their favorite poem and draw a picture of what they are imagining while reading it and post them around the anchor chart.

To introduce a poem, a teacher may begin with a read-aloud. The teacher models how the poem should be read. Students can then read with the teacher as an echo, cloze, or choral read. The echo read is great practice for fluency. Students are simply imitating the way a fluent reader would read each line of the poem. In the cloze technique, the teacher reads the first part of the sentence and students follow along, ready to complete the sentence as an oral read. This technique helps the teacher know when students can actually read the words as sight vocabulary or struggle to decode them. Of course, the choral read can be a fun activity as well. Students can be divided to read different lines or verses. The poem can also be used as the focus of a Your Turn Lesson or mini-lesson in writing workshop.

On the same day or the next day, the poem is read again. Students might draw some sketches of pictures they see in their minds, or retell the poem, or practice a nutshell summary or gist statement. By midweek, the students are reading the poems in pairs. Teachers may conduct a strategy lesson on a literary device or active reading strategy such as making predictions, visualizing, or making inferences. The students may reread to find a strategy they would like to use in writing workshop, and whole-group discussions could center on author's craft. Sometimes, poems could be used with a companion piece such as a picture book, a magazine or newspaper article, or a work of art. On subsequent days, students could write a poem, either individually or collaboratively, that either uses the poem's organizational format, topic, theme, or even a single phrase or word.

# CELEBRATING POETRY

There are many ways to publish poetry—in a class book, on a bulletin board, with a painting, or even performed as a dance, song, or recitation. Poems can be read in different voices or acted out. One poem, or poems paired with students' poems or other works of literature, could be presented in a reader's theater format. Or, students can represent their poems as a painting, clay sculpture, mural, or charcoal drawing to enhance the presentation of the poem(s). They can collaborate to create a collage of all the books and poems they have read and shared that are related to a common theme, topic, or writing structure. Of course, the performances can include both the original poem introduced in reading or writing workshop or the new ones the students have composed. Students can continue to revise and edit original poems or stories, essays, and letters that are connected to their study of a particular poem, pair of poems, or text set that involves companion pieces.

## What Are Companion Pieces?

Companion texts or text sets can help teachers differentiate the needs of their literacy community and help all students find a way to participate and deepen their understanding of concepts, skills, and strategies. For example, students could listen to the Dust Bowl ballads (a poetry form) written and sung by Woody Guthrie at the same time they are reading *Out of the Dust* (a novel written in poetic form) by Karen Hesse or Margot Theis Raven's picture book, *Angels in the Dust*, in literature circles. To introduce yet another format for writing, the teacher may use *Treasures in the Dust* by Tracey Porter, a book written as letters between two eleven-year-olds that give the reader an accurate picture of the Dust Bowl era. Students can imitate first person writing in the persona of a child, man, or woman who lived during this time in history—in the form of a poem, journal entry, letter, memoir, or personal essay—or take a multigenre approach and choose among several forms. *Dust for Dinner* by Ann Turner lends another view for struggling readers and writers. *Children of the Dust Bowl: The True Story of the School at Weedpatch Camp* by Jerry Stanley is a nonfiction selection that can help students write list poems, found poems, and pantoum. The ballads or individual chapter selections from *Out of the Dust* can serve as anchors for the reading of all other kinds of literature and help students write their own free verse poems.

Remember that when we deepen our comprehension—our knowledge or schema—about concepts, people, places, and events in the past or in the present, we essentially pair different experiences together into new understandings and relationships. The insights we gain from pairing poetry with other texts and our life experiences move us toward a deeper understanding of the power, purpose, and significance of poetry.

## Workshop Possibilities

In Lynne's school, some teachers have teamed together to create new opportunities for poetry workshop. Two or three classes at the same grade level introduce possible mini-lessons or Your Turn Lessons using some of the poetry. By the end of the school year, each grade-level folder will contain approximately thirty poems—one for almost each week of the year. The chapters in our book include Your Turn Lessons and activities for each poem. Classroom snapshots take you into our classrooms and guide you through reading-writing connections. The best practices link poetry with vocabulary, fluency, word study, comprehension development, and writer's notebook experiences.

We encourage teachers to continue to add and trade their favorite poems to build a strong collection of mentor poetry. Our work with poetry at Fern Hill Elementary School and the Upper Moreland Intermediate School is building a strong community of readers, poetry writers, and poetry lovers. The staff and students recognize the potential and power of poetry to help us wonder about our world and be joyful.

# CHAPTER 2

# Poetry to Inspire Response

### The Squirrel
*by William Varner*

After we chased the crow away
We went back to check on the squirrel.

She wasn't quite grown
And lay on the dry leaves

Amid the skunk cabbage and ferns
Breathing deeply, slowly, the bone

Exposed on the lower jaw
Blood on its snout like a smeared thumbprint

Small brown eyes mute.
We waited with her until

Her smooth coat rose less and less.
My son and I turned without speaking

And walked back to the house.
We did not see the crow return

To take the body. We did not
Talk about it when we ate.

I heard the sound of light crying
In his room later that night.

Heard him thanking each his stuffed animals
For being things that do not breathe.

In *Speaking of Journals: Children's Book Writers Talk About Their Diaries, Notebooks, and Sketchbooks* compiled by Paula W. Graham (1999), many writers discuss their use of journal writing and make the reading-writing connection. In "More Than Words on Paper," author Mary Jane Miller states that while growing up, books were as important to her as food and eventually brought her to writing in journals (Graham 1999). Mary Jane saves all her journals and at some point in time shifted her routine with journal writing to include three different kinds of journals that she writes in regularly: a gratitude journal, a question journal, and a reflection notebook. Poet Naomi Shihab Nye in "A Constellation of Images" remembers that she began journal writing in second grade. She copied poems into her journals because a teacher had instructed her students to do so in order to increase their vocabulary and learn about how lines were constructed. Later, Naomi used an observation walk with her students to share lists of observations and compare what was noticed or went unnoticed. She states, "One thing that's true about writing: the more we write, the more we have to write. Journals help us remember that motto" (Graham 1999, 206). Author Eileen Spinelli in "Life's Small Moments" talks about her journal writing as a way "to peek through a window to her heart. It is also the window from which she views the world" (Graham 1999, 30). Spinelli buys any books written in journal format. Her advice to young poets and journal writers is to examine the little things. She says that journal writing is helpful because it slows you down and is a place to bring emotions to the surface and explore them.

Reading often serves to evoke strong emotional responses and connections with our experiences. One way to make our thinking visible about comprehension is by teaching students how to make connections that go deeper than scratching the surface. In the case of William Varner's "The Squirrel," students don't need to have had the exact same experience to talk about some kind of loss. Readers of this poem can also explore and connect with the feelings the characters have at different points in the poem by creating a feelings web in their response journals. They could put either "parent" or "son" in a circle in the center of the web and identify the different feelings in words or phrases surrounding the center circle. According to Karen Bromley:

> Webbing encourages student involvement and sharing as you encourage a genuine exchange that reveals rich responses to literature . . . . It promotes and extends comprehension because it allows new information to be related to the known. (1996, 4)

The notebook is a place to explore feelings and thoughts about the world and about the reader's and writer's place in the world. Poetry is extraordinary in and of itself; therefore, it is a great way to inspire written response to reading and original writing. A poem can inspire response in many different forms. It may be another poem, an observation, a list, a personal narrative, a memory chain, a letter, or an essay of advice. Regardless of the form the writing takes, the poem can offer the simple joy of being read aloud many times and should be copied right into the notebook if the author finds the images and words particularly inviting.

In the beginning of the school year it may be helpful to provide a copy of a poem or several poems about notebooks and writing to get students started. Consider Brod Bagert's poem about how he views his notebook:

### My Writer's Notebook

It's a black and white composition notebook,
A hundred pages
with blue line
that await my words:

*Diamond Search*
My life lies before me
Like the bed of a shallow river.
My fingers sift sand and gravel
For the rough diamonds that lie hidden.
And as I find them
I put them in this notebook.
I write . . . I cut . . . I polish . . .
And they shine.

My words on an empty page
In an ordinary notebook,
The silver setting for the jewels of my life.

Bagert's poem begins with a description of a writer's notebook in an ordinary way, but by the end of the poem the metaphor for his notebook is the silver setting that holds all his ideas (his jewels). A notebook becomes extraordinary because of the way a writer makes use of it, returning to it often to find the many colored threads that are repeated in everyday routines and wonderful adventures. The writer's notebook is always a safe place where the writer can choose what he wants to write about, what form he wants to use, and what medium he uses to be inspired: poems, artwork, music, stories, newspaper articles, speeches. Nick Flynn and Shirley McPhillips (2000) view the writer's notebook as a place where students can gather their ideas, try out forms, and practice developing content. Students use their notebooks to study craft from mentor poems used in class, eventually leading them to find their own mentor poems to study and imitate.

An idea you might like to try is to copy small squares of poems such as Bagert's poem or "New Notebook" by Judith Thurman that students can paste into their writer's notebook. Shirley McPhillips (2012) suggests creating folders for a poetry collection that include poems the teacher has shared with the class and other student finds to revisit, read aloud, and discuss with others.

Another favorite is "Writer's Notebook" by Ralph Fletcher:

### Writer's Notebook

My brother Tom says he's a hundredaire
with two hundred fifty dollars
in his bank account.

Dad's a thousandaire.
I gave baby Julia two pennies
so now she's a pennyaire.

When I look at Julia
her little bald head
reminds me of planet Earth.

I put that in my writer's notebook
to maybe write a poem later on;
it feels like money in the bank.

Students may want to create a word web to describe how they feel about their own writer's notebook, the kinds of things they hope to place inside or write about. They can then take a poetry form they are familiar with such as acrostic, haiku, rhyming couplets, or free verse and write a poem about their writer's notebook. Perhaps students can reserve the first page in their writer's notebook for this poem as a way of honoring the notebook itself and immediately making a very personal connection with it.

A work of prose can sometimes inspire a poem in the writer's notebook after discussing a text in reading workshop or another content area. For example, Lynne worked with a group of fifth graders to develop a list of tree words after reading a nonfiction selection, *Autumn Leaves*, by author Ken Robbins. The students were able to visualize each kind of leaf because of the author's use of rich description and similes. Lynne pointed out that her new learning would help her write poetry that she could not have imagined without the help of the list. She used the words from the shared list to compose a haiku in her writer's notebook:

Yellow poplar leaves
Sticking to the wet pavement:
Silhouettes of frogs

Sometimes teachers may decide to ask students to keep a separate reader response journal, and that may be a management or organizational decision. Organization of a writer's notebook should never be so complex that students start to worry more about where to put things than to just write. The notebook is a place to write in daily, perhaps several times a day, to exercise one's writing muscles. These short bursts of writing help students prepare for the longer pieces that require stamina. Whether students study and respond to poems they have read in reading class or another content-area class using a reader response journal or house these entries in their writer's notebook is purely a matter of teacher choice—what works best for the students of a particular grade level.

After creating their tree poems, Lynne's fifth graders were excited to continue to write poetry. In the beginning of the year when students are just beginning to use their notebooks, it is important to give them something concrete and familiar to work with, and it is always a good idea to involve the senses. Poetry shows us how we can start with something very ordinary and write about it in an extraordinary way. Lynne shared the poem "Apple" by Nan Fry that served to help students understand the power of using more than one sense to describe something—in this case, an object—and to demonstrate how something so everyday and familiar can become so unique through the author's words. Lynne brought in different kinds of apples for students to examine and taste. They used a sense chart to record words and/or phrases about apples.

In Lynne's notebook, her senses chart looked like this:

| Sight | Sound | Smell | Taste | Touch |
| --- | --- | --- | --- | --- |
| little brown stem | crispy crunch | sweet | sweet | smooth and hard |
| A precious treasure | | like warm sunshine | tasty and tangy | wet and sticky |
| Round and plump | | natural | ripe | heavy |
| plucked from a tree | | fragrant | rich | round |
| In a salad | | tantalizing odors from Grandma's oven | delightful and delicious | warm or cold |
| Grandma's open-faced pie | | | cinnamon and sugar | |

She used the senses list to create the story poem that follows (the underlined words were inspired by the ideas recorded on the chart).

## A Gift
### by Lynne Dorfman

On this <u>apple-picking</u> day
The apple waits, <u>tempting</u> each passerby.
Its weight tugs on the <u>little brown stem</u>,
The stem, a lifeline to the Mother Tree.

On this warm, apple-picking day,
<u>September's treasure</u> plucked free,
The feel of it, <u>plump and round</u>,
Ready for <u>Waldorf salads</u> or <u>Grandma pies</u>.

On this <u>sweet</u>, warm, apple-picking day
I feel it, <u>heavy</u> in my brown-berry hand,
Heavy with the <u>sweet-tangy juice</u> it holds,
Its <u>crispy crunch</u> contained inside.

The sweet apple, <u>round and ripe</u>,
Ready for me to sink my teeth in,
Hear the crunch, feel the <u>splash of juice.</u>
I cannot wait another moment for this <u>pleasure</u>.

Then a shrill whinny from the chestnut colt,
A beautiful beast with velvet muzzle that
Reaches for this gift in my open palm,
<u>Sticky sweetness</u> spilling between finger cracks.

The slow-moving jaw works the apple bits,
Soft, chocolate eyes revealing pleasure,
A pleasure only a round, ripe apple brings
On this sweet, warm, gift-giving, apple-picking day.

Michael, a fifth grader, had just celebrated the Jewish New Year with his family. He shared the tradition of dipping apples in honey on the night of Rosh Hashanah as part of a memory-writing assignment fashioned around the use of the senses. Michael readily chose apples to create a list and used the information to write a list poem:

Jewish New Year,
Apples dipped in honey.
Halloween and candy apples
Or better yet, caramel dipped.
Dried apples and apple candles,
Giving off crisp scents of autumn.
Applesauce and apple pies,
Apple butter on warm, homemade bread.
Apple for your teacher at year's end,
Sweet memories.

A writer's notebook overflows with snapshots of people, places, and events—small moments in time captured forever on the written page. Our writers can dig deeper and deeper into their minds and hearts—making connections among what they have seen that day, that night, that weekend, or even an entire season—and what memories they recall most readily. A simple scaffold such as "That reminds me" may be all they need to start writing. Consider the images in poet Will Mowery's "That Reminds Me" as a way to get your writers into their notebooks through prose or poetry. (See the Your Turn Lesson about using snapshots of setting at the end of this chapter.)

Poetry should not be reserved for just before the winter holiday and end of school year. Giving students a chance to choose poetry throughout the year to express an emotion, describe a person or place, conjure up a memory, or even to create laughter is giving students the freedom to choose a great variety of topics and forms. If interest in use of the writer's notebook begins to wane, you might turn to poetry to help your students discover new possibilities for their writing.

## CLASSROOM CONNECTIONS:
## POETRY TO INSPIRE RESPONSE

### Pigeons
#### by Charlotte Zolotow

A gray-blue pigeon
blows up his feathers
and struts
across the path
to other pigeons
waiting in the grass.
An old man
scatters bread crumbs
and the pigeons
ripple up to his feet
in a blue and silver wave.

## Reading Connections

Charlotte Zolotow adapted this version of "Pigeons" for *Snippets: A Gathering of Poems, Pictures, and Possibilities* from her earlier work, *The Park Book*, written in 1944. It is a great example of how you can fashion prose into poetry. This poem will help students with visualization. The students can infer the setting using their background knowledge—where they often see pigeons and people feeding pigeons. If some of your students are unfamiliar with a city park or square, you may want to show them some photographs or video clips. The song "Feed the Birds" from the movie *Mary Poppins* may provide a great introduction to this poem. You might ask students to close their eyes while you are reading the poem aloud to them a second time and then turn and talk about the kinds of pictures they are forming in their mind. In order to reference the poem, either post it on chart paper or display it under a document imager. When they are finished talking with a partner, ask the students to share their images in whole group so you can record them on a chart. When you ask students to explain their thinking this helps those students in the class who may have no idea what they should be picturing. It is sometimes not enough to simply tell students to make pictures in their head, they have to be shown how to do that. All students can learn from the thinking of others. Students can then sketch their ideas in their reader response journal.

Metaphor is always a wonderful way to teach students about visualization and inference at the same time. The ripple of the "blue and silver wave" of pigeons helps students picture what that would look like, almost like a movie clip, not a still picture. You might want to ask your students, how can a flock of pigeons be like a wave? Ask your students to evaluate the effectiveness of the metaphor. Compare it to a simple statement such as "the pigeons came up to the old man's feet." What's the difference between the two?

Another powerful reading strategy is self-questioning. Perhaps this is a place where you would want to begin if your students need more work with questioning. As students read "Pigeons" to themselves, ask them to jot down questions that come to mind as they are reading. Be sure to model your own question. For example, your first question might be, "what does 'blows up his feathers' mean?" You can continue this questioning as a shared experience eliciting questions such as "what are the pigeons waiting for?" or "why is the old man feeding the pigeons?" from your students if they are not ready to try it out independently. This self-questioning activity can be carried over to a guided reading lesson and eventually used by students with their independent reading selections.

The wonderful words in Zolotow's piece may lend themselves to exploring words by acting them out. Students can demonstrate what it means to "strut" and even come up with a wide array of verbs that could be used in place of this word, acting each one out to show, not tell, the shades of meaning. Other choices for kinesthetic vocabulary—using movement to act out words and remember their meaning—include "scatters" and "ripple" (of course you will need a group of students to demonstrate this!)

## Writing Connections

"Pigeons" is a great example of close observation, just the kind of entry you hope your writers will have in their writer's notebooks. It is a good example of one small moment in time. You almost feel as if the poet has taken a snapshot and is sharing it with us through words. Students will make good use of writing about settings that embed a character performing an action. These descriptions often serve as great leads for narratives or subjects for songs and poems.

You can invite your students to engage in the same close observation by imitating the work of Charlotte Zolotow. Jason, a fifth grader, wrote a haiku to capture his observation of the wind on the playground:

> Hear kids playing ball.
> The wind brings sound to my ears,
> dries sweat on my face.

> I cannot see the wind
> but I know it is there; pick me
> up and put me down!

Throughout the school year, you can encourage students to find the best in prose by looking for phrases, sentences, or paragraphs that sound like poetry. Students can consider the elements that turn prose into poetry—eliminating unnecessary words, thinking about the length of each line and where best to insert line breaks, the rhythm of the words, and, possibly, considering substitutions for rhyme. They might also consider trying out different punctuation to clarify meaning. In his writer's notebook, Patrick, another fifth grader, wrote about a van in the church parking lot:

> The van is sitting parked with no other cars for miles but just lots of little birds flying over and under leaving "gifts" for the angry owner.

He later went back and fashioned this observation into a poem:

> The van is sitting
> parked
> with no other cars for miles:
> just
> lots of little birds
> flying over and under
> leaving "gifts"
> for the angry owner.

Your writers can see the importance of using strong verbs to help their readers form pictures in their minds. Zolotow uses words such as "scatters," "ripple," "blows up," and "struts" to hold up "Pigeons" and lend detail to a fairly short piece of writing.

Writers might want to notice that Zolotow restates her first line in the very last line (using the color words "gray-blue" as "blue and silver"). The two lines serve as bookends to the piece.

❖   ❖   ❖   ❖   ❖

## Dream Dust
### by Langston Hughes

Gather out of star-dust
　　Earth-dust,
　　Cloud-dust,
　　Storm-dust,
　　And splinters of hail,
One handful of dream-dust
　　Not for sale.

## Reading Connections

At first glance, this poem looks quite simple and straightforward—a short list culminating in the big idea. But it really goes deeper than that, and students may touch only on the surface meaning, interpreting it in a very literal sense.

One way to lead students to a deeper understanding is to pose a question and have students think-ink-pair-share in their reader response journal or writer's notebook. This activity will lead to multiple readings and revisions in their thinking about the poet's purpose and the poem's meaning. You could start by reading the poem aloud to students, then having them read chorally, then having them read it silently on their own. The next step is to ask them to jot down their ideas about the poem's meaning. This might be done in words, pictures, or a combination of the two. Finally, ask students to share their ideas with a partner, then revise their thinking based on what they learned from the collaboration.

You could also conduct a more guided activity by asking students what the title means to them or why the poet remarks that dream-dust is not for sale. Another approach to use would be self-questioning, where the students jot down questions that come to mind as they are reading the poem. These questions can spark rich discussion around many interpretations. The idea is to create a community think tank. This will help you and your students be less afraid of reading poetry, and it may offer some strategies they can use when they are reading independently.

Sometimes, looking at a poem and categorizing the words and images as positive or negative can help the reader dig deeper. For example, "star-dust" would be seen as a positive, where "splinters of hail" could be interpreted as negative. The fact that the poet uses both positive and negative images in this poem leads to more wondering.

Guide students to infer the meaning of the closing thought. "Not for sale" could be followed by "at any price." What makes dream-dust so valuable?

## Writing Connections

After discussing this poem in reading workshop students can turn to their writer's notebook to write about their dreams. What dreams do they have for themselves, their family, the world? They may choose to start with a list, create a web, or dive right in and write their own dream poem or narrative. Your students may want to read other dream poems by Langston Hughes such as "The Dream Keeper," "Dream Variation," and "Dreams" before they write their own notebook entry. Listing and webbing allow the writer to capture ideas that can be returned to and developed at a later time. This is the notebook's true value—a place to store ideas that can be used to write again and again.

As writers students may notice that this poem expresses one thought that makes use of listing things big and small, positive and negative. Challenge your students to write a poem that consists of one complete thought balanced by positive and negative aspects.

If students are drawn to Langston Hughes, he may become a mentor poet for them and they may choose to read more of his poems. Ask students to reflect on the fingerprints—the craft that Langston Hughes employs in his poems. What do they notice that is appealing to them as writers and readers? What do they think they'd like to try out in their own writing?

❖   ❖   ❖   ❖   ❖

### Remembering
*by Patricia C. McKissack*

Mama told me,
"Cloth has a memory."

I hope
the black corduroy remembers
that it was once the pants . . .
my uncle wore to vote for the first time, all clean and new.

I hope
the pink and green flowered tablecloth remembers
the peach cobbler
I spilled on the Fourth of July picnic . . .
before my brother went off to school
in Boston,
when we were still
all together.

I hope
the white lace handkerchief remembers
how pretty my cousin looked . . .
the day she got married to Junior
all over again.

I hope
the dark blue work shirt remembers
how hard Daddy has worked . . .
all his life.

If by chance the cloth forgets,
I want to always remember . . .
all of it.

## Reading Connections

One of the first things most readers do is to make a personal connection with the text, fitting it into their schema. In "Remembering" it will be easy for students to think about what brings back memories to them. They might have a favorite stuffed animal, a piece of jewelry, or a baseball card. Their connection could be about a special place or a special person. It could even be their writer's notebook—a treasure chest of memories. Giving students the opportunity to write about their connections in a reader response journal or a notebook will help them better relate to any discussion of the poem that follows.

"Remembering" provides an opportunity for you to focus on the important skill of visualization with your students. Each verse is like a scene from a movie with different characters and different events. In the context of McKissack's book *Stitchin' and Pullin': A Gee's Bend Quilt*, about quilting and the quilters of Gee's Bend, students can easily infer the meaning and what the poet is experiencing here. However, when the poem stands alone, readers need to create that context for themselves. They first need to imagine where the poet is and what she is doing. The act of visualizing each scene and each piece of cloth will help the reader understand the poem and make meaningful connections. Students can reread each verse silently and aloud and picture what is happening in their head. Then they can either draw some sketches or jot some thinking and turn to share their ideas with a partner or with the whole class. Guide them to find the similarities and differences in their visualizations.

Students can infer who is important to the poet by looking at each verse and thinking about the person and event associated with each piece of cloth. In the first verse, the poet talks about her uncle's going to vote for the first time. Ask students why this memory was included as one of four she wrote about. They may have multiple interpretations. Perhaps they will connect with the excitement of doing something for the first time, or maybe they will think about how important it is to vote. If they have enough background knowledge and know the context for the entire book, they may make the connection to African Americans being given the right to vote. They can deepen their understanding by wondering about the significance of each event.

Poems often use words that are unfamiliar to students. Sometimes the words are old-fashioned, left over from another generation. Explore words like "corduroy," "peach cobbler," and "handkerchief." Words can signal a time period, and students should be made aware of this. The words "memory" and "remembering" lead to word study where students explore related words such as *memoir, reminisce, recollection,* and *remembrance.*

Pointing out the repeated phrase "I hope" can help students organize their thinking. Students will notice that every time the author uses this repeated scaffold a new idea is introduced. You might point out that the first and last thoughts do not use the phrase because they serve as a beginning and an ending.

## Writing Connections

"Remembering" can inspire notebook writing around objects. Although students may not have experience with or connections to a piece of cloth, there are many other objects that will elicit a flood of memories such as dolls, hats, stuffed animals, a catcher's mitt, or a piece of jewelry. Companion pieces such as *Aunt Flossie's Hats (and Crab Cakes Later)* by Elizabeth Fitzgerald Howard, *Small Beauties* by Elvira Woodruff, or *The Memory Cupboard: A Thanksgiving Story* by Charlotte Herman can offer a sea of ideas for poems and stories written around objects.

If students are inspired to write in their notebooks, you could suggest they try out the repeated introductory phrase "I hope" or suggest something similar such as "I remember." This writing may first take the form of a paragraph and later be revisited and rewritten as a poem if the student chooses. Or you can start by asking students to draw a series of boxes each containing the scaffold that is going to be repeated with enough room to sketch the memory in detail. Students can take their most vivid memories and write the words to match.

This poem, along with the book it is in, provide an opportunity for students to understand how Patricia McKissack gathered research to write a book of poems around quilting. Here is a chance for students to create an authority list if they don't already have one. An authority list is an expert list of topics that students can dip into for writing. We all have things that we like to do or know a lot about. Students could consider gathering more information about a topic such as skateboarding, fly-fishing, or caring for a pet. This information may be transformed into poems, stories, or reports.

This poem gives us a chance to look at interesting leads for poems. McKissack starts with a dialogue lead that sets the stage for the rest of the poem. Without the lead there would be a loss of meaning. This poem also has a satisfying ending that voices what the writer is thinking and feeling.

Of course, you can look at the use of the ellipsis to convey the lost-in-thought feeling of the poet, and her choice of simple adjectives that do not overpower the memory of the actual event. Also, McKissack makes use of proper nouns such as Fourth of July, Junior, Boston, and Daddy. These words lend specificity to the poem, which makes it more real and personal.

❖　❖　❖　❖　❖

## Every Time I Climb a Tree
### by David McCord

Every time I climb a tree
Every time I climb a tree
Every time I climb a tree
I scrape a leg
Or skin a knee
And every time I climb a tree
I find some ants
Or dodge a bee
And get the ants
All over me

And every time I climb a tree
Where have you been?
They say to me
But don't they know that I am free
Every time I climb a tree?
I like it best
To spot a nest
That has an egg
Or maybe three

And then I skin
The other leg
But every time I climb a tree
I see a lot of things to see
Swallows rooftops and TV
And all the fields and farms there be
Every time I climb a tree
Though climbing may be good for ants
It isn't awfully good for pants
But still it's pretty good for me
Every time I climb a tree

## Reading Connections

"Every Time I Climb a Tree" is a great poem to foster fluency in your students. This poem uses the repetition of the phrase "Every time I climb a tree" to create a beat or rhythm. This is an example of a chant poem, a poem that does not have a fixed form but that repeats one or more lines again and again and begs to be read aloud. The absence of punctuation marks (except for two question marks) gives the reader a feeling of breathlessness and excitement. And that is the way this poem should be read—in an explosion of words. To do so, students will need to be able to quickly recognize the words, so it helps them to develop a stronger sight vocabulary. Unless your students are very young, you may want to call attention to some words such as *dodge, scrape, swallows,* and *awfully.* Here is an opportunity for some decoding instruction. The rhyming words help students predict what the words will be and can lead to instruction with word families and the different spellings of long "e" at the end of the word.

This poem also lends itself to lessons on compare/contrast structures. McCord includes both good things and not-so-good things that happen when climbing a tree. To make this structure more visual for your students, a simple T-chart works well with this poem. It might look something like this:

| Not-so-good things about climbing trees | Good things about climbing trees |
| --- | --- |
| scrape a leg<br>skin a knee<br>dodge a bee<br>get ants all over me<br>parents ask where I've been<br>rip my pants | feel free<br>spot a nest that has an egg<br>see things like swallows,<br>rooftops, fields, and farms |

Students can use the chart to paraphrase the poem and write a summary in their response journals of the bad and good things about tree climbing listed in the poem. You could ask your students to close the paragraph by explaining how the poet evaluates tree climbing in the last two lines. Readers can think about the poet's final thought to determine point of view. Who might have a different point of view about climbing trees and why?

Students can infer who is speaking in the question, "Where have you been?" This is an excellent time to point out that an inference uses knowledge from the text and from the student's schema. The great thing about this is that there is room for interpretation. The speaker could be a parent, a grandparent, or any family member. While not all students may have experience with tree climbing, they have all been lost in a favorite activity where a good amount of time passes without their even knowing it. Students can infer why the poet feels free when tree climbing and think about what activities give them a sense of freedom. Students can also infer the setting for this poem. If the poet can see "all the fields and farms there be" he's probably not in a city or even the suburbs. Finally, when the poet tells us that tree climbing "isn't awfully good for pants," students can infer what happens to his pants when he climbs trees.

## Writing Connections

This poem can inspire students to write notebook entries around things they like to do. After reading the poem several times, ask your students to think about the things they do almost every day or the things that make them feel free. In one first-grade classroom, Rose and the students brainstormed ideas such as walk the dog, play with LEGOs, play football, go to recess, skateboard, go to the park, and walk home. After modeling her own poem about walking the dog, she and the students decided to create a shared poem about going to recess. First they created a T-chart where they listed the good things and the not-so-good things that might occur on any day at recess. Here's what they came up with:

| Good things that happen at recess | Not-so-good things that happen at recess |
| --- | --- |
| score a goal | scrape my knee |
| make a new friend | get mulch in my shoe |
| jump fifty-two times before missing | didn't get picked for the game |
| get picked first for the kickball game | fall off the swing |
| run around with friends | get pushed |
| play football | get a nosebleed |

Together they then wrote a shared poem around the repeating scaffold "Every time I go to recess":

Every time I go to recess
Every time I go to recess
Every time I go to recess
I fall off the swing
Or get pushed on the blacktop
But every time I go to recess
I get to play kickball or football
And make new friends
Every time I go to recess

It is important not only to model for the students but to also engage in shared writing experiences. Most students need this scaffolded instruction in order to be successful independently. After the shared writing, the students discussed their ideas with a partner (oral rehearsal is a great form of prewriting), then spent the rest of writing workshop drawing pictures and creating their own poems (see two examples in Figures 2.1 and 2.2).

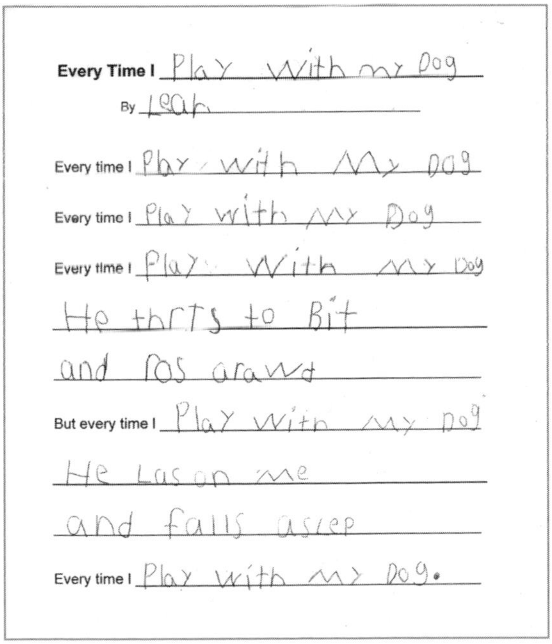
Every Time I Play With my Dog
By Leah
Every time I Play with My dog
Every time I Play with my Dog
Every time I Play With my Dog
He thrTs to Bit
and ros arawd
But every time I Play With my dog
He Las on me
and falls asleP
Every time I Play with my Dog.

**Figure 2.1** Leah, grade one, uses "Every Time I Climb a Tree" as a mentor poem.

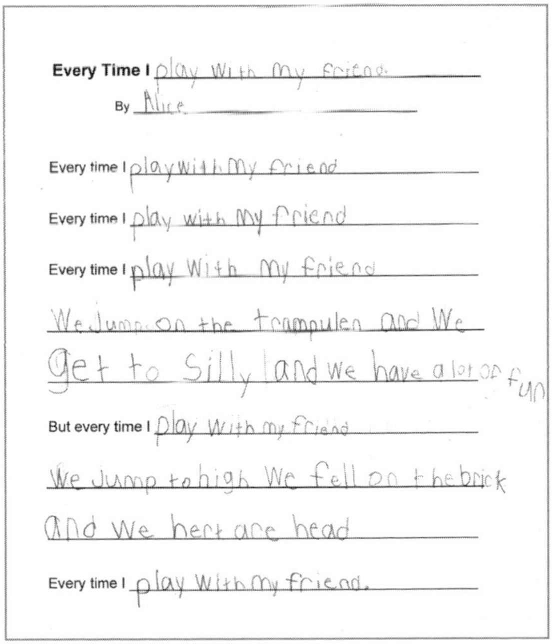
Every Time I play With my friend
By Alice
Every time I play with my friend
Every time I play with My friend
Every time I play With my friend
We Jump on the trampulen and We
get to Silly and We have a lot of fun
But every time I play With my friend
We Jump to high We fell on the brick
and We hert are head
Every time I play With my friend.

**Figure 2.2** Alice, grade one, uses "Every Time I Climb a Tree" as inspiration for her "Every Time I Play with My Friend" poem.

You might discuss with older students how the absence of punctuation in this poem is very purposeful. One thing for your students to consider is how punctuation or the absence of punctuation affects the pace of the poem and rhythm of the words.

The effective repetition holds the poem together and helps emphasize that this activity (tree climbing) is done often. Writers can look for other poems and children's books that make use of effective repetition, copying examples into their writer's notebooks and reflecting on the purpose that is served.

❖   ❖   ❖   ❖   ❖

## Summer Squash
### by Donald Graves

"Just a 'no-thank-you' helping,"
my mother choruses from the kitchen.
I sit alone at the table
with a mound of summer squash
on my plate; the kind of squash
with yellow warts, seeds, and white guts.
I lift my fork but my nose says,
"Smells like vomit" and I drop
the mass to my plate.

I sit alone, long after my brother
has eaten the cursed concoction.
He leaves with a grin
knowing I'll sit and suffer
until I eat one forkful.
Father and Mother look kindly
at Brother who loves vegetables
just because I don't.

Mother wants to finish
the dishes and raises a forkful
to my straight-lined mouth.
"Open up, now!" she orders.
The watery mash with seeds
and strings enters my mouth;

I prepare to swallow, push
my head forward, breathe
deeply, and hold the mix
in my mouth waiting
for Mother to leave.

I cough and spit the poison
to my plate and call my dog, Rags.
First, I give her two pieces
of meat and she begs for more.
I slip in a forkful of squash
in rhythm with her expectation.
She drops the bite to the floor,
shows the whites of her eye, then trots into the living room.

## Reading Connections

"Summer Squash," like William Varner's "The Squirrel," could be referred to as a story or narrative poem. It has all the elements of story: characters, setting, problem, events, and possible solutions that the reader must imagine based on what he has read and what he knows about the characters. Students may draw the conclusion that the poet may be in even more trouble with his mother at the end. When a reader has a story map in his head as part of his schema he can read any kind of narrative and know how it's supposed to go. The story map helps the reader make good predictions and organize his thinking.

This poem uses colorful language like "cursed concoction," "choruses," and "no-thank-you" to describe the size of the helping of summer squash. "Poison" is used metaphorically to clearly let the reader know just how much the poet detested the vegetable. Students may not be familiar with these words, or may know them in other contexts or as other parts of speech, so here is an opportunity to do some vocabulary work.

This narrative poem gives us many opportunities to make inferences. As readers we will think about the relationship the poet has with his brother, noting that the brother's name is not used, but he refers to him as "Brother." As students visualize this scene, they can use the words to infer how much time has passed. The poet helps us to do this by repeating "I sit alone" in separate verses. In the last verse, students can use inference to understand that the dog is expecting another piece of meat instead of the "no-thank-you" helping of squash that she gets.

## Writing Connections

Many students will want to try out the narrative poem. There are many other great narrative poems such as "The Highwayman" by Alfred Noyes, "Casey at the Bat" by Ernest Thayer, "The Owl and the Pussycat" by Edward Lear, and "Hiawatha's Childhood" by Henry Wadsworth Longfellow that can be on hand for students to read. In their writer's notebooks students may want to think about a vivid memory they have that basically has a beginning, middle, and end and could possibly be formatted as a poem. One way to find these stories might be through a memory chain (a stream of consciousness where writers start with a word such as a season, a holiday, a favorite person or place, or an object and record a chain of thoughts that are evoked). Students might want to divide a page in their writer's notebooks into four quadrants for each season and record moments that come to mind. They might also quickly jot phrases or even sentences that come to mind about events that occurred with a person they spend a lot of time with to be able to lift one and create the story poem. Here's an example from Lynne's notebook:

**Mom and Me**
➢   Coloring in books when I was sick
➢   Chasing my sister and me around the dining room table
➢   Walking with my sisters and me to the library on Wadsworth Avenue
➢   Ordering cheeseburgers and milkshakes at Barson's Restaurant and being caught by Dad
➢   With me for my "first" driving lesson
➢   Trying to bake Grandma's famous apple pie

Some students will have an easier time if they write the experience as a personal narrative first, then go back and change it into a poem by considering line breaks, punctuation, the most necessary words, and rhythm.

Rose was looking through some of her old notebooks and came across a short narrative about a coat she made for her daughter one Easter. She could see on the previous notebook page that this entry had come from an event listed in a memory chain. As she read through the narrative, she decided it might work well in poetry form, so she rewrote it using "Summer Squash" as her mentor poem:

### The Coat

"Easter in March—
It will be cold!"
I think to myself
as I envision Annie's Easter outfit
in my head.
A coat will be just right,
I decide.

I find the perfect fabric—
a twill of royal blue
with a soft silk blend for the lining.
Slowly, the coat takes shape
as the fabric glides effortlessly
through my sewing machine.
The finished product fits her perfectly!

Easter morning dawns
sunny, clear—
and hot!
A sultry eighty-five degrees!
Much too hot for a three-year-old in a coat.
As I approach she gives me a
you've-got-to-be-kidding look.
But before she can protest,
We line up to take a picture.
Click! The coat will live on.

The sprinkling of dialogue and thoughtshots help Graves' poem (and Rose's) take the form of a story and make it more inviting for the readers. Students sometimes include too much dialogue in their narratives. "Summer Squash" is a great model to show students that less is more.

There are also great examples of rich descriptions (the squash and the dog). The telling detail about the dog ("shows the whites of her eyes") gives the reader enough to picture a dog in their minds. The poet's description of summer squash is enough to make anyone not want to eat it. It is particularly effective that the description in the first verse is carried into the third verse as well.

This poem has voice—it sounds like a young boy who is eager to do things other than sit at the table and eat summer squash. Ask students to consider how the poet's choice of words helped create this honest, tell-it-like-it-is, no-nonsense voice. Even his simple use of capitalizing the word "Brother" and never using his brother's first name lends voice to this piece. His commentary ("Father and Mother look kindly at Brother who loves vegetables just because I don't") is not a necessary piece of the story, and yet it gives us that inside information and makes us chuckle.

## Your Turn Lesson

# WRITING AROUND AN OBJECT TO REMEMBER

Writers often use concrete objects to make connections with events, people, and places in their lives. Sometimes a concrete object helps a writer create a time line of memories around something specific such as Christmas, Thanksgiving, the first day of school, or summer vacations.

**Hook:** Reread "Remembering" by Patricia McKissack. Talk with your students about how the pieces of cloth helped the poet visualize and re-create a memory. In this poem, the cloth elicits a snippet of memory tied with emotion. You might point out to your students or allow them to discover that the poem uses personification . . . it is as if the cloth remembers. In addition to the companion pieces mentioned in the chapter, other options include *The Best Part of Me* by Wendy Ewald and the poems "Keepsake" by Eloise Greenfield, "Teddy Bear Poem" by Judith Viorst, "A Book" by Myra Cohn Livingston, and "Marbles" by Valerie Worth.

**Purpose:** *Sometimes writers need to begin with a concrete object in order to jog their memories to create notebook entries that will inspire poems and stories. As you can see, Patricia McKissack has used the pieces of cloth that will make a quilt to write about many different ideas. Today we are going to make a list of objects that might help us do the same thing. McKissack begins her poem with some dialogue: Mama told me, "Cloth has a memory." Let's use that scaffold and brainstorm possibilities.*

**Brainstorm:** Ask students to make a list in their writer's notebook that could complete the phrase "_____ has a memory." Have them turn and share their list with a partner and again in small group. This can also be done as a whole class with students sharing orally and the teacher charting responses.

A list might include a baby blanket, a teddy bear, sneakers, a baseball, a house, a kitchen table, a piece of jewelry, a hockey stick, a piece of clothing.

**Model:** Choose one item from the brainstormed list and demonstrate how you could use this object to remember small moments. Think aloud as you write. You can borrow McKissack's scaffold of "I hope" to begin each description or change it to something else such as "The _____ remembers." Here's an example from Lynne's notebook:

I hope my sneakers remember the time I lost one
of the pair in the Devon Horse Show mud while
trotting a horse to the gate of the big riding ring
under the lights on a dark rainy night, my heart
pounding in my chest.

I hope my sneakers remember the time I left
them at Grandma's because Mom had threatened to
throw them out. But Grandma saved the day by soaking
them in her wash tub and scrubbing them until they
almost looked brand new.

I hope my sneakers remember how I cried when my
feet had finally outgrown them and I had to part
with my lucky shoes.

**Shared/Guided Writing:** The easiest shared experience to explore with students is to use an example from the classroom such as the teacher's desk, the classroom walls, the door, or the class pet. Together with your students create some memory snippets. Remember it's not important to tell an entire story here. These pieces of memories will evoke other writing in many different forms. As students share a piece of a small moment, record it on chart paper. You might want to use a different color for each snippet so students can easily see that each snippet stands alone and may not share a space in time with each other.

**Independent Writing:** Students can return to the list created in their notebook or the shared brainstorm list and choose one to write from. It might be helpful to ask students to bring in an object and do this independent writing the next day. Remind students that linking the object with a strong emotion or one of the senses can help them spill memories more easily. For example, "I hope my sneakers remember walking to school" will not provide enough information to launch a specific memory, but "I hope my sneakers remember walking to school when the neighborhood bully tried to steal my lunch box and my sneakers dashed across the yard to safety" will paint a much clearer picture.

**Reflection:** Ask students to think about how this strategy worked for them:

*Was it easy or difficult to write around an object?*
*Will you be able to use a snippet from your entries to create a story or poem?*
*Can you write a remembering poem like McKissack's using your snippets?*

**Option:** Now that these rememberings are part of their notebook, students can use them as a jumping-off point to write a story, poem, or letter.

## Your Turn Lesson

# USING SNAPSHOTS OF SETTING TO MAKE MEANINGFUL CONNECTIONS

The ability to make meaningful connections is important to both the reader and the writer. Our storehouse of memories that we draw from in order to write fluently and effectively about the people and places we love are often scattered throughout our notebooks in the form of snapshots of setting. We write across the seasons, we write across day and night, and we write across the passing years. Snapshots are usually very visual at first but also can include other senses such as sounds and smells. In "That Reminds Me," poet Will Mowery uses snapshots in a unique way to create a poem that helps readers to visualize his experiences and make meaningful connections to anchor these images.

### That Reminds Me

I was sitting by a stream
    when I saw a grasshopper hop from a rock
        and land on the other side
And it reminded me of how we used to jump
    across the puddles in the driveway
        after a summer rain—
            except the grasshopper didn't get all wet—
    and didn't get the giggles

I was sitting on the porch
    when I saw a squirrel in the weeping willow tree
        vaulting through the air
            to another limb
And it reminded me of how we used to tie ourselves
    into the low branches of that tree
        and run
            and swing
                up off the ground
We were like flying squirrels

> I was lying on my back in the grass
> > when I saw a maple leaf fall off a high branch
> > > and float in the wind
> > > > out past the top of my head
> And it reminded me of the time our kite string broke
> > and the kite soared out over the top of the hill
> > > and we never saw it again
>
> I still think about that old kite
>
> And it reminds me of you

**Hook:** Read "That Reminds Me" by Will Mowery and make a list of the images that students remember after you finish reading the poem aloud. For younger students give them time to draw some of the things they are seeing in their mind. You can talk about how writers paint pictures with words and help readers visualize people, places, and actions. Discuss with your students how the poet used strong verbs and appealed to the senses and emotions to create vivid descriptions. Point out how each snapshot served as a catalyst to trigger a personal memory. Companion pieces for this poem could include *The Listening Walk* by Paul Showers, *The Goodbye Walk* by Joanne Ryder, and *The Listening Walk* by David Kirk.

**Purpose:** *Writers, today I am going to show you how to create a poem using a series of snapshots of setting that you will record in your writer's notebooks over a period of days that will help trigger connections to other memories.*

**Brainstorm:** Using their notebooks students will make notes and sketches about their environments. You can take them on nature walks around the school or even within the building. Here is a perfect opportunity to do some writing at home. Students can sit on their front stoops or backyard patios and record their observations in words and/or sketches. Encourage students to label their drawings and use all their senses to take in the settings they are observing. Chart a common list in school during writing workshop. Urge your students to describe in phrases and sentences rather than one-word lists and be sure to include your observations as well. Entries might include things like:

three lonely empty swings
plump morning doves nibbling food around the feeder
an American flag flapping in the wind
a slender garden spider weaving a pattern across the blades of grass

If your students bring in one-word lists (squirrels, spider, birds), you can encourage them to expand their thinking by asking questions so that the complete image is recorded on the class chart. "Squirrels" might become "Squirrels were running up and down the tree."

**Model:** Take one of your ideas from the chart and model for the students how you would first describe the setting and then make a meaningful connection to another memory. Here's an example:

> I was walking by the playground
> And I saw three lonely empty swings
> Waiting for children to pour out of the school at recess.
> And it reminded me of how I kicked my legs back and forth
> and propelled myself through the air,
> higher and higher
> And I felt as free as a bird.

**Shared/Guided Writing:** Together with your students create an additional poem around a familiar school setting. Choose an observation from your class chart and provide a sentence stem such as "I was standing (or sitting, or walking, or playing)." Have your students create detailed images and use questioning to help them find those details. Once they have a vivid description, they can think about a connection to another memory anchored in sensory detail or feelings. Here's an example from a third-grade class:

> I was strolling through the hall
> and I noticed two boys sitting silently
> on the bench outside the principal's office.
> And it reminded me of sitting silently
> on the bench in the grassy field,
> watching someone else
> score the winning goal in the soccer match.
> I still think about that game.

This shared writing experience may need to be repeated until you are sure your students understand the process.

**Independent Writing:** Invite students to compose their own poem using snapshots from the chart or from their notebooks. Encourage them to link two or three experiences, first describing through the senses and then linking to another memory.

**Reflection:** Ask students to reflect on how the snapshots helped them to make connections with other memories.

*What strategies did you use to create a vivid snapshot?*
*Was it easy to make a connection after writing your description? Explain.*
*Could any of your descriptions be improved by using a different sense?*
*Do you appeal to the reader's emotions?*
*How does making meaningful connections help you in your reading?*

**Option:** Students could return to their poems during another writing workshop to write the story behind the memories recorded. In the shared example just given, there may be a story behind the soccer game and the reason why the player was sitting on the bench.

# List Poems Are for Everyone

**Walking Home from School I See:**
*by Rebecca Kai Dotlich*

A bus with a flat tire.
Pennies in a puddle.
Baby birds.
Fat worms.
A crooked gate.
A mailbox spray-painted pink.
A bulldog wearing a raincoat.
A bumblebee.
A reflection in a window—
me!

Listing is a very accessible form of poetry for all writers. It is a way to record ideas and make thinking permanent, and it almost always begins with observing. Consider the poem by Rebecca Kai Dotlich. Students in every grade can make a list of things they observe on their way to and from school. It doesn't matter whether they are walkers or bus riders! A list like this can be written for every season. Students can notice how as readers of this poem they must make inferences to draw the conclusion that the setting is a rainy day in spring. As good detectives they will notice the description of the bulldog dressed in a raincoat and puddles on the ground. The bumblebee, baby birds, and fat worms all say spring! Dotlich creates a positive, happy tone—a pink mailbox, the possibility of good-luck pennies nestled in a puddle, and the poet's surprise and excitement of discovering herself in a window reflection.

Listing is a natural part of the prewriting experience. When students make lists it frees them up to think about the range of possibilities without worrying about sentence structure, grammar, and punctuation. After the list is created teachers can show students how to revisit it to notice patterns. Writers can be encouraged to organize their list around a theme, essential question, or point they are trying to make. Additionally, the list should be sequenced in a logical, meaningful order. Students may need to revise to achieve the best order. Certain lines could be repeated for emphasis. Finally, another consideration involves the length of the line and the rhythm of the lines as they are read aloud. Some ideas for list poems include:

➤ things I don't know
➤ things I don't do
➤ noisy things
➤ quiet things
➤ scary things
➤ things that drive me crazy
➤ thing I can't understand
➤ spring things
➤ things that melt my heart
➤ things that are happening in the world at this very minute

One spring, the kindergarten classes in Rose's school were engaged in a science unit on butterflies. They were also once again getting outside to revel in the warm air and notice other changes in nature. By this point in the school year they understood the difference between a letter and a word, and they were not afraid to put their thinking on paper. The stage was set to introduce them to poetry, and what better way to start than with a list poem.

Rose and the kindergarten teachers began by sharing lots of list poems with the students. Doug Florian's "What I Hate About Winter" and "What I Love About Winter" were perfect examples of recording thoughts as a list. The children could easily relate to Rebecca Kai Dotlich's "Lost and Finds," a list poem that describes the contents of a box of treasures. "Spring" by Lee Bennett Hopkins was the perfect mentor poem for showing these young writers that their observations of the world could be recorded as a list and read as a poem. After several days of observing signs of spring, collecting ideas and words, and crafting a poem together, the students were ready to write (see examples in Figures 3.1 and 3.2).

Liam chose to use the list poem to tell a story. That morning in writing workshop all the students were trying out list poems. Liam was very excited to tell about the rivalry between the bluebirds and the chickadees in his backyard. Rose suggested he write about it, but Liam was reluctant. He wanted to try out the list poem and didn't quite know how to tell his story in that way. With some guidance from Rose, together they recorded phrases and Liam crafted a list poem story (Figure 3.3).

**Figure 3.1** Sam's list poem about spring

**Figure 3.2** Kylie combines ideas in her list poem about spring: Wind blowing trees/Grass blowing in the breeze/ And the bright blue sky.

**Figure 3.3** Liam's list poem: Bluebirds/Chickadees/Fighting/For the/Nest/Chickadees/Won/I love/Spring

In one third-grade class, students wrote list poems about collections they have at home. In order to get started they brought in a few items from their collections and talked about them with a partner. They all started their list poems with the same first line, imitating their teacher's model. Amy wrote about seashells:

> Amy collects shells
> Shells with bumpy edges,
> Shells with pink inside,
> Amy loves shells,
> Shells, shells, shells, shells:
> White like the moon,
> Bright orange like the sun,
> Little and white like the clouds,
> Amy collects shells!

Both Georgia Heard (1989) and Ron Padgett (1987) note that the list or catalog poem has been around for centuries. In fact, you can find examples of list poems in Book II of Homer's *Iliad* and the Bible's book of Genesis. In *Poetry: Starting from Scratch*, Michael Carey (1989) often uses this kind of poem in an assignment format called a "things to do poem." He considers this kind of poem to be a variation of a "Happiness is . . ." poem (you can substitute any emotion such as loneliness or anger). "Useless Things" by Richard Edwards in Paul Janeczko's *Poetry from A to Z: A Guide for Young Writers* will show students how a list poem can be unique and include outside-the-box thinking. After all, everybody makes lists. From food shopping to bucket lists, everybody makes lists!

*Falling Down the Page: A Book of List Poems,* edited by Georgia Heard, is a rather complete source of this type of poem for students of many ages. It is a collection of list poems from different poets written in different formats. Heard uses cooking terms for her poem "Recipe for Writing an Autumn Poem." Here is an opportunity to have students read cookbooks to get the feel of the structure, acquire the proper nomenclature, and apply it to the subject they are writing about. Lee Bennett Hopkins writes a question poem in "Why Poetry?" J. Patrick Lewis writes "What Is Earth?" a question poem that provides a possible answer for each question (see Chapter 1, "Getting Started," for a discussion of question poems). Other poems are written as persona poetry or "how to be" poems, such as Bobbi Katz's "Things to Do If You Are the Sun" and Elaine Magliaro's "Things to Do If You Are a Pencil." As you can see, Heard's collection will keep you and your students busy for a long time.

The poems in this chapter will serve as resources and models for your students as they hear, read, share, and explore possibilities for reading and writing list poems.

## CLASSROOM CONNECTIONS: LIST POEMS

**Signs**
*by John Frank*

Songbirds hushing,
Maples blushing,
Rivers rushing—
Fall is here.

## Reading Connections

A natural way to begin exploring any poem is to think about how you can use it to practice fluency. "Signs" offers young readers a rhythm for speaking and reading. The use of noun-verb phrases for three of the four lines helps beginning readers establish a sense of phrasing that fosters reading fluently for meaning, instead of merely reading without comprehension in a word-by-word fashion. After modeling what a fluent reader sounds like, students can chorally read the poem several times until they are able to read it themselves. Display the poem on large chart paper for the entire week so that students can continue to read it as a class, with a partner, or independently. Students can be asked to find letters or words to extend their understanding of the alphabetic principle and build a beginning sight vocabulary. Fluency can also be fostered by providing practice in a listening center where students can hear their voices and/or your voice reading the poem.

We often use word families to help beginning readers consolidate sounds. Looking at the rime in "hush," "blush," and "rush" will help students begin to use skills in phonemic awareness and phonics to read through the word.

Specific nouns such as "songbirds" and "maples" and unique verbs such as "hushing" and "blushing" offer opportunities not only for vocabulary development but also for visualizing. When students visualize images as they hear or read the poem, they are forming their own interpretations and understandings. Sometimes it helps young readers to draw a picture about what the words help them see and feel as they hear the poem. In *Reading with Meaning: Teaching Comprehension in the Primary Grades*, Debbie Miller (2002) discusses how readers' images and understandings are influenced by sharing the thinking of others. After drawing, ask students to turn and talk with a partner about their pictures and the words that inspired them. By sharing their ideas with a partner and then drawing again students learn how important it is for readers to think about what they are reading and let others' thinking in to clarify understanding. Finally, they can compare their pictures to that of the poem's illustrator, Mike Reed. Not only are students developing a love of language, but they are also learning how words help readers to visualize and comprehend.

Students can use the title, "Signs," to help them make predictions about the subject of the poem. They can also begin to see how to synthesize ideas to draw a conclusion. This simple poem presents three details and ends with the main idea.

## Writing Connections

This poem has a simple organizational scaffold that writers can easily imitate. It is a list poem that lists three details in noun-verb sentences and concludes with the statement of the main idea. A good companion text—a picture book written in this sentence structure throughout—is *Snowsong Whistling* by Karen Lotz. Writers can brainstorm signs for other seasons and apply it to this scaffold. For example, in one first-grade class, students did a shared writing after brainstorming signs of winter.

> Snowflakes falling,
> Fires crackling,
> Bears hibernating—
> Winter is here.

Notice that the rhyming aspect of the poem was not part of the scaffold. Rhyming can limit the scope of a young writer's thinking, although some young writers may be ready to try it out. The scaffold and/or brainstormed list can then be offered to writers as an option for independent writing. (See the Your Turn Lesson at the end of the chapter.)

Although the poem offers a study in the use of commas, periods, and the dash, don't be too concerned if your writers don't use these tools. Some may be ready and may naturally use the punctuation marks as they imitate the scaffold. That is the perfect time to have a conversation about what they are and why the author used those marks. You could also just concentrate on one, such as the period, if your students are beginning to understand and use it.

For older students, return to the poem and examine each line as a way of introducing or reviewing the use of auxiliary or helping verbs. Students can take lines from *Snowsong Whistling* as well and practice writing lines of poetry as complete sentences by adding the present or past tense of helping verbs that are needed with the "–ing" form of the verb ("Maples blushing" could become "Maples are blushing."). As another option, you can show your students how to change the "-ing" form of the verb to other forms. For example, "Maples blush" or "A maple blushes." For more sophisticated writers, you might have a discussion about the use of fragments like "maples blushing" or "rivers rushing" that are purposefully placed for emphasis or rhythm within a narrative or another genre that uses paragraph form instead.

Make a reading-writing connection by talking about word choice—particularly, the specific nouns and verbs. It is a good idea to point out that the poet probably purposefully chose the verb "rushing" (instead of, perhaps, "gushing") to describe rivers in order to create alliteration. Ask your writers to notice other examples of this craft as they begin to understand the importance of sounds in language.

Writers often appeal to the senses to help their readers anchor images in their mind. You can point this out to your students as they brainstorm words for their own writing. Use simple headings such as I see, I smell, and so on, as students seek words for their own writing.

❖    ❖    ❖    ❖    ❖

### Zeke, an Old Farm Dog
*by Kristine O'Connell George*

The black dog on the knoll is my dog:
Sailing over construction fences,
Chasing bulldozers,
Barking at butterflies,
Swimming in the neighbor's
New backyard pool.

Now he steals things
And brings his prizes to the front porch:
Sunday papers and other dogs' pans,
Shingles, keys, someone's ham on rye.
I won't fence him in.
I won't even try.

## Reading Connections

"Zeke, an Old Farm Dog" offers students a chance to explore unique words such as "knoll" and "rye" and to ponder words that are traditionally used as nouns, such as "construction" and "Sunday," but whose meaning changes slightly when used as adjectives. What do we think about when we see the noun "Sunday"? Perhaps going to church or family dinners come to mind. But using "Sunday" to describe a newspaper conjures up images of our favorite comic strips, ads for stores where we might shop, or our favorite section of the paper, like the sports page.

Of course, we can practice reading this poem aloud and develop a cadence for reading two verses that contain colons and lots of commas. Students practice reading the punctuation and notice that the pace of events—the things happening in the lists—are read more quickly in the second verse because of the way the activities are grouped together rather than listed on each line.

The poem gives us a chance to visualize scenes in the dog's life. We can see Zeke flying over fences, swimming in the neighbor's pool, or snitching the Sunday paper. To teach students the importance of visualizing as they read, you could ask them to draw scenes from each of the verses. These scenes can also be used as a sequencing activity for students who need practice with that skill.

This poem offers excellent opportunities to demonstrate to readers how thinking critically about words and structures deepens their comprehension. Begin with the word "old" that appears in the title and discuss its importance to the poem. This one word allows readers to better understand why the author compares and contrasts the activities of Zeke as a young dog and then as an older dog. The transition word "now" helps the reader infer that Zeke as an older dog is still engaging in mischievous activities, although they are tamer and require less exertion. The last two lines demonstrate the poet's point of view. A rich discussion can follow about what the poet is thinking and whether you agree with her. This kind of thinking and discussion will help students understand the main idea of the poem.

## Writing Connections

This poem demonstrates how the colon can be used effectively in a poem to create lists. Talk with your students about the use of commas and end punctuation. These lists are built without the use of any conjunctions. Try reading the poem and add *and* to each item in the list. Discuss how this change affects the rhythm and meaning of the poem. Without the conjunction, the poet is asking the reader to imagine much more than what is said. The list doesn't stop here as it does when you add the word *and*.

Notice the verbs in the "-ing" form that begin the lines of poetry in the first verse. By beginning with these verbs the poet emphasizes the actions and gives you a feeling that they are happening as she is telling you about them. Writers can try out this technique in their own poetry, beginning lines with strong verbs in the "-ing" form.

You might point out to your students how the poet helps the reader focus on the action by sparsely using ordinary adjectives and how the use of specific nouns and verbs limits the need for adjectives and adverbs. Sometimes writers use a familiar word as a different part of speech to make their readers think a little harder. For example, in this poem, "fence" is used as a verb instead of a noun. Also, "construction" is used as an adjective instead of a noun. You could ask your writers to collect sentences from their reading experiences that use ordinary words in an unexpected way and add them to their writer's notebook to perhaps apply to a future piece of writing.

❖   ❖   ❖   ❖   ❖

## Orders
*by A. M. Klein*

Muffle the wind;
Silence the clock;
Muzzle the mice;
Curb the small talk;
Cure the hinge-squeak;
Banish the thunder.
Let me sit silent,
Let me wonder.

## Reading Connections

Fluency is always a good place to begin with poetry. By reading the poem aloud in many different ways, students become familiar with its language and rhythm. Students focus on the punctuation—semicolons, commas, and periods—to practice fluency as they read the poem aloud. Multiple readings improve both fluency and comprehension. This poem lends itself to reading aloud alternately between two groups of readers. For example, boys could chorally read the first line and girls could chorally read the second line, and so on. The last two lines could be read in one voice by everyone.

For younger readers, who are developing decoding skills, pointing out how to break apart the two-syllable words ("muffle," "muzzle," "thunder," "banish," etc.) can help them add to their reading strategies. This poem also offers the opportunity for teaching or reviewing the different sounds of "c" and long and short vowel sounds for "u" and "i."

"Orders" is a gold mine for word work because it uses many unusual verbs that students may not be familiar with, or verbs that more often appear as nouns, such as "curb" and "muzzle." Students can look for synonyms for these verbs or create a homonym study.

As with many poems, "Orders" is rich in opportunities for extending comprehension. It lends itself to a discussion surrounding the main idea and where it can be found in this particular poem. In a list poem, the poet often saves his point of view or main idea for the final line or lines. Students might ask, "Why are these orders being given?" The answer is the main idea—the poet wants quiet in order to think and wonder. A poem's title is almost always a clue to its meaning. Students often tend to skip titles or not spend much time thinking about them because they are unaware of their importance. You might ask your students to offer an opinion about the title. Is it a good one? Why or why not? You can then ask them to revisit the title and rename it to capture the poem's essence. In one third-grade class, poet readers came up with these alternate titles for "Orders": "Quiet!"; "Let Me Wonder"; "Hush"; "Quiet, Please!"; "Shhhh . . . I'm Thinking."

Many students do not automatically form pictures in their minds as they are reading texts, although once they are taught how to do this and practice, it soon becomes second nature. Poems are a great way to teach visualization because they are short. You may want to ask students to use the clues in the poem, the specific orders the poet is giving, to imagine where the poet is. Have them draw a picture of that place and share their drawing with a partner.

## Writing Connections

In any piece of writing, the verbs are the muscles that hold it all together. This poem uses strong and unusual verbs to begin each line of poetry. These verbs also help the reader understand that imperative sentences (commands) are being used with "you" as the understood subject. The poet changes not only the sentence structure for the last two lines but also the punctuation (from a semicolon to a comma) perhaps to signal that the poem is coming to a close and that there is an important shift. You can talk to your students about when to use this type of sentence; in addition to poetry, imperative sentences easily fit into a process or "how-to" piece or an essay giving advice.

You could also collect lines of poetry or other texts (such as *Painting the Wind* by Patricia and Emily MacLachlan) that make use of the semicolon in a list and discuss how its use changes the way the line is read and the meaning ever so slightly. Gathering lots of examples and creating an anchor chart that displays mentor sentences is an excellent way to conduct a study of punctuation.

Another possibility is to explore the use of the hyphenated word to create an unusual noun ("hinge-squeak"). The author has given a name to a sound for a squeaky door. By doing so the poet has demonstrated economy of expression and created something unique at the same time. Ask your students to read similar writers and find other instances of hyphenated words used as nouns, verbs, and adjectives. For example, the name of a flower, "snow-on-the-mountain," in *The Divide* by Michael Bedard and the use of an original verb and noun in *Langston's Train Ride* by Robert Burleigh: "I skit-skat a little half-dance on the sidewalk."

Of course, students can use "Orders" to brainstorm a list of commands they would like to give and write a poem around their list, concluding with the reason why they are giving the orders. Another possibility is to make a list of small wonderings—things they would like to sit and wonder about.

❖     ❖     ❖     ❖     ❖

## Swift Things Are Beautiful
### by Elizabeth Coatsworth

Swift things are beautiful:
Swallows and deer,
And lightning that falls
Bright-veined and clear,
Rivers and meteors,
Wind in the wheat,
The strong-withered horse,
The runner's sure feet.

And slow things are beautiful:
The closing of day,
The pause of the wave
That curves downward to spray,
The ember that crumbles,
The opening flower,
And the ox that moves on
In the quiet of power.

## Reading Connections

This poem illustrates how comfortable Elizabeth Coatsworth was in writing about the world of nature. Although written in 1934, "Swift Things Are Beautiful" offers images that are still inviting to students today. Even on a first read, students need to read the punctuation in order to use proper phrasing and expression. You can ask students to look at the end of each line and note whether it has a mark of punctuation. Each verse contains a thought that requires two lines, and the reader needs to keep reading to get the full meaning; for example:

And lightning that falls
Bright-veined and clear,

This poem offers students a chance to explore the meanings of words and how adjectives are created and matched with their nouns. What images are conjured up by "bright-veined" when describing lightning? What is the implied metaphor here? You might ask your students to come up with other synonyms that describe lightning. Another hyphenated adjective to ponder is "strong-withered." The reader must have some knowledge of a horse's anatomy to understand the specificity and perfectness of this adjective choice. Horses' withers are the strongest part of their backbone. You can point out to students how important it is to develop background knowledge and to widen their schema in order to develop a deeper understanding of text. Students might explore the idea of "sure feet" and what makes them swift. The vocabulary might also offer the reader clues about the setting—when and where the poem was written.

"Swift Things Are Beautiful" can also present opportunities to teach inference: What is the meaning of the poet's last thought?

> And the ox that moves on
> In the quiet of power.

In order to understand these lines, students must be familiar with what oxen are and what they do. Otherwise, you may want to turn to pictures or the computer for help. This will enable students to understand that power does not always have to be fast or loud, that strength can be as quiet as an ox pulling a farmer's plow.

Another way to deepen students' comprehension is by having them order the images the poem evokes on a continuum, from swiftest to slowest. As they evaluate each, they might add other ideas.

## Writing Connections

The vocabulary in this poem easily bridges reading and writing workshops. With your students, take a second look at the hyphenated adjectives ("bright-veined" and "strong-withered") and the nouns they describe. Chart the other nouns in this poem and, as a writing community, brainstorm hyphenated adjectives to go with them; for example, rip-roaring rivers, rush-gushing rivers, lacy-fingered wave, or just-blossomed flower. Ask students to return to one of their notebook entries, either a poem or prose, and find a noun that needs an adjective. Students may try out hyphenated adjectives that give specificity and originality to a piece of their writing.

You may explore the importance of word choice—making every word count—by creating adjective pairs that are opposite in meaning and asking students to brainstorm words that mean the same or nearly the same as each adjective and its antonym. Students can use them to describe nouns and write a similar two-verse poem following the scaffold of "Swift Things Are Beautiful."

In one fourth-grade classroom, the students wrote a whole-class poem comparing "big" and "little" around things in a city.

Big things are beautiful:
Billboards and bridges,
And skyscrapers that disappear
In New York City smog,
Concrete mixers and front-end loaders,
Double-decker buses,
The Statue of Liberty,
Sprawling Central Park.

And small things are beautiful:
The sidewalk cracks,
The rooftop gardens
That city-dwellers love,
The long-handled pooper scoopers,
The apartment complex elevators,
And the one bedroom studios
In rented-out buildings.

Of course, "Swift Things Are Beautiful" also offers a chance to study alliteration, the use of colons, commas for listing, and the repeated use of "the" to mark the noun that follows.

❖   ❖   ❖   ❖   ❖

## Helping Hands
### by Allan Wolf

Hands are for taking.
Hands are for holding.
Hands are for shaping
and paper plane folding.

Hands are for grasping.
Hands are for shaking.
Hands are for touching
and shadow-play making.

Hands are for dressing,
buttoning, zipping.
Scrambling, buttering,
flapper-jack flipping.

Hands are for clapping,
juggling, jiggling.
Hands are for washing
and brushing and wiggling.

Hands are for raising,
writing and talking.
Catching and throwing
and bright sunlight blocking,
wringing and twisting
and turning and knocking.
Clock hands are perfect
for ticking and tocking.
But up-side down acrobat hands
are for walking.

## Reading Connections

"Helping Hands" is a great choral read because it uses effective repetition and has a definite rhythm and rhyme scheme. Teachers can have fun with this poem, rereading it as an echo or cloze read. Different groups of students can be assigned to read a verse of the poem aloud. Another option is to encourage students to put some hand motions into their oral reading of the poem.

For young readers, the syllables can be clapped out as the teacher reads. This activity can help establish an understanding of sound units (or phonological awareness) that are a foundation for successful reading. In addition, pointing out the end rhyme pairs can segue into the creation of word families. For example, in the first verse "holding" and "folding" provide the rhyme for eventually recognizing the "old" word family. Words such as these can be used to start anchor charts that students can add to throughout the year.

Young readers can also benefit from examining the spelling patterns for words in the "-ing" form. Many of the words in this poem are consonant-vowel-consonant plus silent "e" words ("take," "shape," "make"). Students can practice reading words in their base form and "-ing" form, then find other examples in their independent reading and writing. Engaging students in word awareness activities such as charting will help them make discoveries on their own about how our language works. By charting the different "-ing" words, they may begin to see a pattern that will lead them to create a rule as to when to double the final consonant.

The kinesthetic vocabulary in this poem gives students a chance to employ their many different learning styles to understand and remember the words' meanings. Words like "zipping," "grasping," "brushing," and "wiggling" might inspire students to come up with a motion or gesture that suggests a definition for the word. Their classmates might respond by repeating the word, tracing its spelling in the air, performing the motion, or devising one of their own.

"Helping Hands" lends itself to beginning lessons on making inferences. Almost every student can understand what "bright sunlight blocking" would look like by using their hands. Ask them to show, not tell, this action and to look around the room at what their classmates are doing. They will discover that everybody is doing about the same thing. How did they know what to do? They used what was in the text plus what was in their head (their schema) to discover meaning. In other words, they made an inference. Again, asking students to think about what hands would be doing when they are "scrambling" or "buttering" will lead them to discover that the hands are preparing breakfast. They will then more easily understand that "flapper-jack flipping" refers to making pancakes, even though "flapper-jack" is a word created by the poet.

To further comprehension, you might return to the title and ask students why the poem is named "Helping Hands." They can also come up with alternative names for the poem and justify their thinking.

## Writing Connections

As with other poems we have suggested, verbs play an important role in "Helping Hands." Even though the poem is built around one word, *hands*, it is the verbs that create the images and provide the backbone of the piece. You can point out to students how important it is to choose verbs wisely. The verbs in this poem are not necessarily unusual, but they provide the strong visual images that the author wants to convey. Students can return to pieces they are currently working on or to previously written pieces and examine the verbs they used for possible revision. Perhaps a different verb could provide a stronger image. It is a great lesson in revision to show the difference one word can make.

"Helping Hands" follows a fairly predictable scaffold, but a few surprises can be found along the way. We usually think of words such as "acrobat," "paper plane," "shadow-play," and "flapper-jack" as nouns, but here they are used as adjectives. This adds interest to the poem—as does the somewhat surprising ending that changes up the scaffold just enough to keep the reader thinking.

Students can easily use "Helping Hands" to help them compose a text innovation focusing on another body part. Two great companion pieces to use for such an activity are *Here Are My Hands* by Bill Martin Jr. and John Archembault and *The Best Part of Me: Children Talk About Their Bodies in Pictures and Words* by Wendy Ewald.

"Helping Hands" could also provide inspiration for some students to express what they learned in a book like *What Do You Do with a Tail Like This?* by Steve Jenkins and Robin Page that explores the things animals do with their tails, eyes, ears, mouth, noses, and feet.

## Your Turn Lesson

## USING A SCAFFOLD TO WRITE A LIST POEM

Scaffolds provide a framework for writers to organize their thinking. The structure that an author uses can be a repetitive word, phrase, or line that sometimes introduces a new idea and sometimes restates an important idea for emphasis. In poetry, scaffolds appeal to our sense of sound as we read the words silently or aloud. Just as we look for patterns in nature, we search for them in our writing.

**Hook:** Return to "Signs" by John Frank and discuss the scaffold the author uses. Help your students discover that the poem consists of noun-verb phrases followed by a main idea. (You may need to explain the difference between a noun and a verb if your writers are very young.) Companion pieces that use the same scaffold include *Snowsong Whistling* by Karen Lotz and *Moon Glowing* by Elizabeth Partridge. You can also find examples of the two-word scaffold in *Pumpkin Eye* by Denise Fleming, but the order is changed to adjective-noun ("swooping bats," "hissing cats"). Notice that these "–ing" words denote action but answer the question "What kind?" This book can offer an alternative scaffold to some students.

**Purpose:** *Writers, today I am going to show you how to create a list poem using two-word phrases. We'll also be thinking about the main idea we want our readers to understand about our topic so that we can choose the best words to support that idea.*

**Brainstorm:** Together with your students brainstorm a list of topics they could easily use. Seasons and holidays work well with this lesson, but your list might also include animals, sports, or any other topic your students have some knowledge of. Choose one and brainstorm nouns and verbs that come to mind to describe your topic. You may have more than one verb for each noun. Brainstorming as many words as possible will give you and your students lots of choices. Be sure to record your verbs with the "-ing" ending. Create two columns (nouns, verbs) on chart paper or the whiteboard to use as a resource. Here's an example:

| Nouns | Verbs |
| --- | --- |
| flowers | nesting |
| birds | building |
| tulips | growing |
| buds | chirping |
| robins | returning |
| butterflies | spreading |
| bluebirds | hopping |
| daisies | flitting |

As you collect words from your students, tease out more specific nouns and verbs from the general categories they may give you. For example, if a student gives you "flowers," put it on the list to honor his suggestion, but your next question might be, "What kinds of flowers do you know?" This charting provides a chance for you to also work on synonyms. If a student offers "sings" you might ask for other words that describe the sounds birds make. Another possibility is to look for word combinations that provide alliteration. Students can use thesauruses and dictionaries to find interesting words.

**Model:** Talk with your students about how you first want to think about your main idea, or what you want your readers to understand about the topic. Following the scaffold, this will be the last line. Explain to them that deciding on your ending thought will help you choose the words and ideas that go best with your poem. For example: *I think spring is such a beautiful season* so *I'm going to make my last line: "Spring is beautiful!"* Continue to think aloud as you choose the words to create your poem. A finished example might look like this:

### Spring

Tulips blooming,
Dogwoods budding,
Daffodils glowing,
Spring is beautiful!

You can stay with the scaffold of four lines or add additional noun-verb lines to offer more choice to your students.

Here's another example from Rose's notebook that uses the adjective-noun scaffold:

## My Busy Garden

Nesting bluebirds,
Chirping chickadees,
Hovering hummingbirds,
My busy garden!

**Shared/Guided Writing:** Together with your students create an additional poem using their ideas. You can keep the same main idea or change it. Be sure to engage in lots of thinking aloud about word choice. Before students write individually you can return to other topics and continue to brainstorm additional words. For example, if you are writing about seasons you might want to brainstorm words for all the seasons so students have more choices. One way to do this is to post charts and have students work in small groups to record the words on the charts. They can rotate among the charts in carousel fashion to continue to add ideas.

**Independent Writing:** Invite students to create their own list poems using the words charted or on a topic of their choice. As an option for young students, this activity can be part of a reading and/or writing center. Write the words on oak tag strips and place them in two columns (nouns/verbs) on a pocket chart. Students can rearrange the words to create list poems then practice reading them for fluency, or they can record them in their writer's notebooks.

**Reflection:** Ask students to reflect on how creating the list poems worked for them:

*How did the use of the scaffold help you with your writing?*
*How did choosing your main idea first guide your word choice? Why is this important?*
*What other topics could you use in creating this type of poem?*
*When might you use this scaffold again?*

## Your Turn Lesson

# USING THESAURUSES AND DICTIONARIES TO WRITE A LIST POEM

In poetry, word choice is so important. Poets are wordsmiths, masters of their native language. We search for good words in our writing. One of the most powerful ways we have to revise is to go back and look at our words to decide if we could choose more specific ones. The greater the vocabulary at our fingertips, the more powerful our writing can become. Students need to be familiar with the thesaurus and dictionary and must practice replacing words in their stories, poems, and reports for more desirable ones. Work with synonyms and antonyms will help students become wordsmiths.

**Hook:** Read "I'm Talking Big!" by Colin McNaughton and discuss the words the author uses to get his point across to the reader. Help your students discover that the poem contains synonyms for the word "big" that indicate varying degrees of bigness. (You may even want to list some of these words and ask students to help you place on a continuum on the board or chart paper to make it more visible for them.) A companion piece that can be used to stimulate interest in the poem, find new words, or rewrite the poem with nouns is *How Big Is It?*, a cool nonfiction book by Ben Hillman that explores the concept of big with incredible photos and wonderful descriptions.

### I'm Talking Big!
*by Colin McNaughton*

I'm talking big!
I'm talking huge!
I'm talking enormous, immense,
Tremendous!
I'm talking hulking, towering,
Titanic, mountainous!
I'm talking maximum, massive,
Stupendous, gigantic, monumental!
I'm talking fantastic, fabulous,
Incredible, unbelievable, mammoth,
Vast!

I'm talking astronomical, mighty,
Monstrous, universal, colossal,
Magnificent, galactical!
I'm talking BIG!

**Purpose:** *Writers, today I am going to show you how to create a list poem using adjectives that are synonyms. We'll also be thinking about how these words mean nearly the same thing but have different degrees of intensity, so the meaning really is slightly different depending on which synonym we choose to use. We want our readers to understand our message regardless of what we are writing about or what genre we choose to use, so we need to choose the best words possible to support our big idea.*

**Brainstorm:** Together with your students, brainstorm a list of words that easily lend themselves to synonyms, such as *weird* or *fast*. You could use Ben Hillman's books, *How Weird Is It?* or *How Fast Is It?* as read-alouds (you don't have to read the entire book because it is so easy to dip in and out of Hillman's books), or you might choose words like *hungry, angry, sad, clean, happy,* or any other words your students have some knowledge of. Choose one, say, *hungry,* then brainstorm all the synonyms that come to mind for that word (*empty, voracious, starving, famished, ravenous, eat-a-horse, wasting away*). Students can discuss shades of meaning as the list is being created. Brainstorming as many words as possible will give you and your students lots of choices. You might want to work with two separate words so that later on you can do one as a shared experience and allow the students to partner to work with the other word as a guided experience.

As you collect synonyms from your students, tease out more, interesting words by allowing them to work with thesauruses and dictionaries.

**Model:** Talk with your students about how revision is a way to honor a piece of fine writing. Many times we do the work of substitution, removing general or worn-out words from our writing. This revision sharpens our piece of writing and helps us write with clarity. You can stay with the scaffold of the fifteen lines from McNaughton's poem or shorten it up to give students a taste. It might be a good idea to practice one in your own writer's notebook before modeling in front of your students, or keep a good thesaurus handy. Use of the computer thesaurus and dictionary is also a great way to model how to do this electronically. Some students have never used a thesaurus, even by the fifth grade!

Here's an example from Lynne's notebook that uses McNaughton's scaffold and the use of synonyms to create a list:

## I'm Talking Weird
### *by Lynne Dorfman*

I'm talking weird!
I'm talking strange!
I'm talking odd, unusual,
Extraordinarily extraordinary!
I'm talking unique, curious,
Peculiar, bizarre!
I'm talking alien, foreign,
Unknown, uncanny, never-seen-before!
I'm talking out-of-this world, incredible,
Unbelievable, unimaginable, abnormal,
Uncharacteristic!
I'm talking mysterious, supernatural,
Irregular, unconventional, atypical,
Creepy, eerie!
I'm talking weird!

Compare your poem (or Lynne's) to McNaughton's poem. Talk about the effective repetition in this poem and the use of hyphenated adjectives such as "never-seen-before" and "out-of-this-world" as well as the adverb adjective pair "extraordinarily extraordinary" (see Margie Palatini's *Mooseltoe* and *Moosetache* for the "perfectly perfect" phrase as a model) in Lynne's version. You might want to talk about the use of commas and exclamation marks as well as line breaks.

**Shared/Guided Writing:** Together with your students, create an additional poem using their ideas about another adjective such as fast or slow. (Or try both!) Be sure to engage in lots of thinking aloud about word choice. Students can brainstorm with a partner or small group before you call on them to write on chart paper. Make sure lots of dictionaries and thesauruses are on hand. Post blank pieces of chart paper and have students work in four or five separate small groups to record the words on the charts. They can rotate among the charts if the words are different in carousel fashion to continue to add ideas or you can ask students to reference all the charts (if they are about the same word) as you write the shared poem together.

**Independent Writing:** Invite students to create their own list poems using a word of their choice and its synonyms.

**Option:** For younger students, this poem can be created around the nouns in one of Ben Hillman's books or a topic they have already studied and researched in a content area. For example, students may have studied a biome, a period in history, a genre such as mystery, or even a planet. Here is an example from a third grader at Lynne's school:

### I'm Talking Mars!
*by Zach*

I'm talking the red planet!
I'm talking polar ice caps, cave entrances,
Extinct volcanoes.
I'm talking Mars!
I'm talking fourth planet from the sun,
Orbited by two moons,
Named for the Roman god of war.
I'm talking Mars!
I'm talking the most Earth-like seasons,
A subject for myths,
Possible colonization,
Earth's hopes and fears . . .
I'm talking Mars!

**Reflection:** Ask students to reflect on how creating the list poems around synonyms worked for them:

*How did the use of the McNaughton's poem help you with your writing?*
*How did the use of a thesaurus or dictionary help you? Did you use any other sources?*
*What other topics could you use in creating this type of poem?*
*When might you use this adjective-synonym poem again?*

# CHAPTER 4

# Acrostic Poetry: Accessible and Challenging

**ACROSTIC**
*by Will Mowery*

An acrostic poem
Contains words that
Rely
On the title or subject to
Show what
The poem
Is trying to
Communicate

Poet Will Mowery describes the acrostic as both accessible and challenging for poets at any level. All too often acrostic poetry is filled with thoughts that either do not relate well to the topic of the poem or are completed with words that relate to the topic but convey disjointed ideas. Consider the difference between these two poems about recess:

## Recess

Running
Everybody plays
Children
Extra time outside
Swings
Slides

## Recess
### by Will Mowery

Ready to relax,
Everyone?
Come on out;
Enjoy some fun.
Swing and play and
Skip and run.

The first poem is simply a listing of words or disjointed ideas. It doesn't have a point or a "so what?" The readers are unsure what they should be thinking about or who the voice is behind the words. In the second poem, the author conveys an idea about recess as something that is relaxing and inviting through his word placement and his use of punctuation. Equally inviting is his use of rhyme. We can hear his voice.

Many poems have a particular shape or form. These poems include the limerick, haiku, tanka, cinquain, and concrete poems to name a few. The acrostic poem is held together with the placement of the letters of the word that spell out the topic or idea in a vertical fashion. In order to write wonderful acrostics students need great models and many shared writing experiences. There are several ways to approach the writing of an acrostic.

One way is to develop a huge word bank built around one topic or idea in the form of a list, word storm, or word web. Students can draw from these graphic organizers or lists to create their acrostic. When they are grasping for a particular word to match a letter that starts a line of poetry, older students can easily rely on a thesaurus, dictionary, or rhyming dictionary for help.

Sometimes students can use an informational book or even a textbook if the acrostic relates to content-area material. While working with a fifth-grade class, Rose demonstrated how to write an informational acrostic using ideas found in *A Butterfly Is Patient* by Dianna Hutts Aston. Each two-page spread of this book describes a butterfly in a certain way, then presents information to further explain the description. As a model, Rose chose the page describing the butterfly as scaly. Using the information accompanying this description, she composed the following acrostic:

Shiny, stacked scales
Cover butterfly's wings
Attracting mates or
Lapping up the sun's heat as butterfly
Yearns to take flight.

The class then examined the page "A butterfly is helpful," and together they wrote this shared acrostic:

Hovering in the garden, the butterfly
Enjoys sipping nectar,
Landing lightly on each flower as
Pollen clings to its body, then
Falls away,
Ultimately producing seeds for
Long-lasting garden beauty.

When we ask students to synthesize information they have learned to create something original, we are providing opportunities for them to use higher-order thinking skills. An original poem (or piece of prose) can easily be used as an alternate form of assessment in the content areas. See the Your Turn Lesson: Writing an Acrostic Poem Around Strong Verbs at the end of the chapter for more ideas about creating informational acrostics.

You could also take your topic and write as many words as you can think of for each letter you are using. You and your students can think about the topic and ask some questions to help you think of more words. Why is this topic important? What would my students/classmates want to know about this topic? Why do I enjoy studying/learning about/thinking about this topic? Think about this topic by exploring the five senses.

In Mrs. Moore's third-grade class, the students studied the acrostics in *Silver Seeds* by Paul Paolilli and Dan Brewer. Lynne and their teacher, Mickey Moore, guided the students to notice things about these poems and list them on an anchor chart:

- ➤ The poems helped readers to form a picture in their mind just like a photo.
- ➤ Each acrostic could be read as one or possibly two thoughts about one topic.
- ➤ Some poems were just a rich description.
- ➤ Verbs were often used in their "-ing" form.
- ➤ Appeal to the senses was often onomatopoeia or taste.
- ➤ The lines were connected and used punctuation including commas, ellipses, and periods.

Since it was December, Lynne and Mickey decided to work with winter words. Starting with the word *winter*, the students worked collaboratively as a whole group to brainstorm words for each letter. They were recorded on large chart paper. For example, for the letter *w*, the young writers came up with: *wonderful, white, wonderland, waves, wild, woods, would, when, where, withered, with, while, won, wake up, weather.* The letter *i* was more difficult. Lynne and Mickey explained that this line could simply serve to connect a thought in the first line with another idea in the third line. They offered *in, if, into, inch, idea, intelligent, interesting, icicles,* and *igloo.* Students actually asked to use dictionaries and thesauruses; and although some students needed help or found words that would be hard to use, it was all about an enthusiasm and excitement for words and finding the perfect ones for the shared poem. The following poem is the result of several attempts. Punctuation was considered after the poem was written. The class talked about using ellipsis points, a dash, or a colon at the end of the fourth line, and the students liked the dash.

> **W**hite snowflakes falling from the sky
> **I**n piles and piles and
> **N**o one is willing to go
> **T**o the playground today—
> **E**ven school is closed.
> **R**iding sleds will be fun!

Of course, many students chose to write holiday acrostics independently. Mickey and Lynne created a bank of holiday words and urged the students to make a list of word choices for each letter of the acrostic word they chose. Many students wrote about winter sports as well. Melissa wrote:

> **F**antastic frost on a
> **R**emarkable day reminds me
> **O**f a snowman
> **S**inging carols
> **T**o surprised
> **Y**oung children!

In March, students returned to acrostics to write about spring things. They created an anchor chart with topics, sometimes listed as a single word and sometimes listed as a phrase. Students were encouraged to start out with an acrostic about spring and narrow their focus to a picture they could form in their mind about a spring activity, scene, or event. Lynne chose Ron Hirschi's book *Spring* as the mentor text, and students found what sounded like poetry to them even though this book is written as prose. Acrostic poetry books were also available for students to browse including Steven Schnur's books on the seasons. Lynne and Mickey advised the students not to write about many different things, but to represent spring through a narrow lens, zooming in on something fairly specific. Jacob knew what he wanted to write about: barbeques! Mickey and Lynne knew that the letter *q* would be a problem, so they asked the class for help. The students used different dictionaries and pulled out words such as *quiet*, *quite*, *queen*, *quick*, *quill*, *quip*, and *quintuplets*. Nothing seemed to fit. Then one of the students suggested, "quarter" and Mrs. Moore exclaimed, "Quart!" Then Jacob knew what he would write for that line of poetry. Here is Jacob's poem:

**B**ig juicy steak
**A**nd buttered corn on the cob melt in your mouth.
**R**ibs with sweet
**B**aby Ray's sauce are
**E**xcellent additions.
**Q**uarts of apple cider drip from the jug and
**U**nder the table, Angel
**E**ats the leftovers off of people's laps!

In Connor's poem (see Figure 4.1), his use of sports as his topic word allowed him to write an acrostic list poem about his favorite sport, baseball. Notice his use of the colon to signal a list is coming. Mikey (see Figure 4.2) made use of alliteration and appealed to the sense of touch in his poem about spring. We loved his choice of the verb "nibble" to describe the biting insects!

In Jon DeMinico's class, the students used spring things as a topic for a warmup. Together,

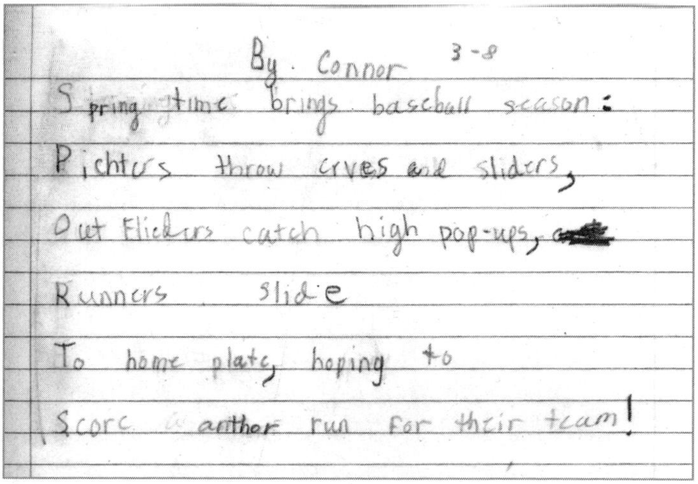
By . Connor 3-8
Spring time brings baseball season:
Pichturs throw crves and sliders,
Out Flickers catch high pop-ups,
Runners slide
To home plate, hoping to
Score anther run for their team!

**Figure 4.1** Connor's acrostic about baseball

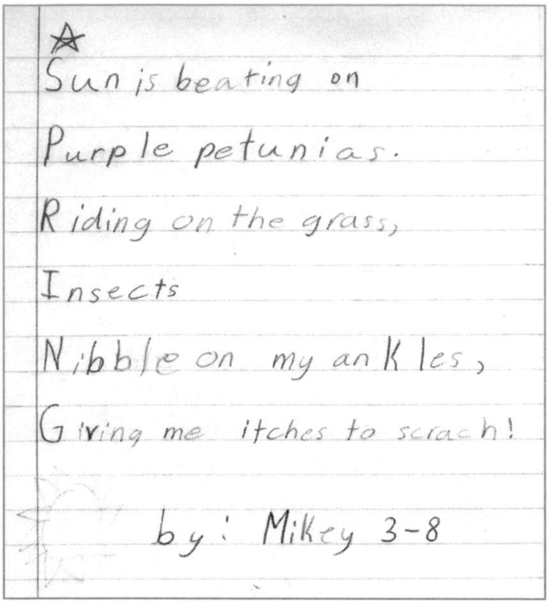

☆
Sun is beating on
Purple petunias.
Riding on the grass,
Insects
Nibble on my ankles,
Giving me itches to scrach!

by: Mikey 3-8

**Figure 4.2** Mikey's spring acrostic

they brainstormed a list of spring things and revised for specificity. For example, instead of the word *flowers*, students named flowers from their gardens: crocuses, daffodils, daisies, roses, petunias, and hyacinths. Mr. DeMinico revisited a mini-lesson on adjectives used after the nouns they describe and used the poem "Moon" from Paolilli and Brewer's *Silver Seeds* as a model. Students chorally read several poems from this text and noted the use of personification and appeal to the senses. Lili wowed us with her poem:

**S**tupendous
**P**etunias, preferably purple or pink,
**R**ising high
**I**n the sky!
**N**ow they are free . . .
**G**alloping as if they had legs!

The class turned their attention to the writing of an acrostic poem in the form of a definition. They used "Idle" in Schnur's *Summer: An Alphabet Acrostic* as their mentor poem. This poem does not offer a formal dictionary definition; rather, it gives us two good examples of what it means to be idle. Jon has had a routine in his class for the past four years. When the students come in, there is a new word-of-the-day on the board. The students try to pronounce it, and then Jon writes it in a sentence so students can try to discover the meaning through context. They look it up in dictionaries and try to write their own sentences. Jon challenges them to use the word throughout the day in reading, writing, science, and social studies classes. Whenever it is possible, Jon uses the word, too. It seemed like writing definitions in the form of an acrostic poem would be another way to reinforce the use of the word-of-the-day. To demonstrate, Jon used a simple and familiar word, *school*, to create a definition acrostic poem (see Figure 4.3). He asked the students to think about the poem and wrote down their noticings on an anchor chart (see Figure 4.4).

After writing several poems together, the students worked independently to write definition acrostics. Here is Elizabeth's poem, also making use of forms of other word-of-the-day words such as *perseverance, flabbergast, accomplishment*, and *aspect*:

Persevering proud young denizens
Really flabbergast adults. Whether it's
Outside or inside, they
Demand accomplishment
In every aspect,
Gaining fame as a
Youthful expert.

Although Connor's poem is simple, he clearly defines his word in his poem:

To work very hard,
Out of school and
In school.
Lots to accomplish!

Kelly tackles *sagacious*, a difficult word for a third grader. She relates it to school work and what she knows best:

Saying and knowing all the
Answers—making denizens flabbergasted with
Grand
Addition and subtraction problems and huge
Conundrums. Always solving
Impossible predicaments, doing an
Outstanding job,
Utilizing wisdom and
Showing hard work!

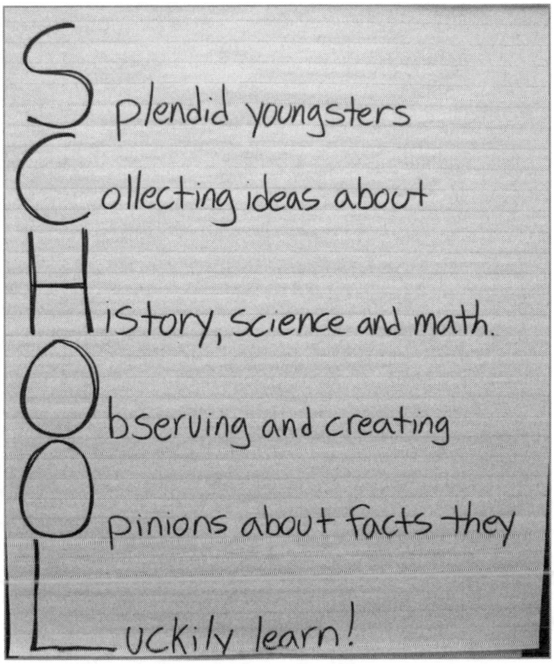

Another way to approach acrostics is to write down your thoughts about the topic. Then find a way to revise your thinking by using the acrostic structure and adding punctuation, such as a commentary dash, an ellipsis, a colon, or a semicolon. End punctuation can also be used when the poem needs more than one sentence to create the big idea. Students can experiment with connecting words, such as conjunctions, and other sentence structures that

**Figure 4.3** Definition acrostic poem model

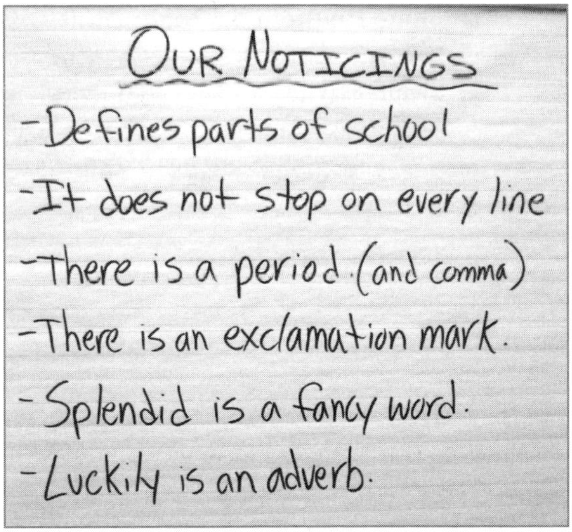

Splendid youngsters
Collecting ideas about
History, science and math.
Observing and creating
Opinions about facts they
Luckily learn!

OUR NOTICINGS
-Defines parts of school
-It does not stop on every line
-There is a period. (and comma)
-There is an exclamation mark.
-Splendid is a fancy word.
-Luckily is an adverb.

**Figure 4.4** Anchor chart of students' noticings

may include the use of dependent and independent clauses. Of course, for those students who love rhyme and can use it fairly well, the acrostic will present a new challenge.

Acrostics have been around for a very long time. In David Hummon's book *Animal Acrostics* we learn that some of the Psalms are really abecedarian acrostics (acrostics that begin each line with a successive letter of the alphabet from *a* to *z*) that were based on the twenty-two letters of the Hebrew alphabet. Look at other books such as *Animalia* by Graeme Base and *Animal Alphabet* by Bert Kitchen to find other abecedarian acrostics. A wonderful example, "Wintering Over," appears in *The Monarch's Progress: Poems with Wings* by Avis Harley.

Steven Schnur has written four acrostic books around the seasons, using the alphabet to organize his ideas. It is interesting to note that many of his acrostics are short, comprised of four lines of poetry. They make excellent examples for students who are trying to write an acrostic that is one complete thought but spans four lines. A number of his poems are written around a word that creates a metaphor. (See "Jewel" later in this chapter.) Clearly, his poems are wonderful resources for vocabulary growth and exploration—particularly his wonderful verbs. Now here's a big surprise: Schnur begins each of his books with an acrostic poem that describes a beginning. For example, *Autumn: An Alphabet Acrostic* begins with a poem about an acorn, the beginning of an oak tree. In *Winter: An Alphabet Acrostic*, Schnur begins with a poem about dawn and starting a new day. *Summer: An Alphabet Acrostic* opens with a description of setting that focuses on new life. Each book moves gradually through the season and ends with acrostics that hint of the next season.

*Silver Seeds* by Paolilli and Brewer is a beautiful book that uses acrostic poetry to describe an entire day from dawn to nightfall. The illustrators, Johnson and Fancher, complement each poem with a beautiful painting that spans two pages. The similes and metaphors are vivid and easy for students to understand and imitate.

While acrostics may appear simple, they can provide challenges to students in both reading and composing them. But the benefits are well worth the effort.

## CLASSROOM CONNECTIONS: ACROSTIC POETRY

### Butterfly

Bobbing
Up and down;
Twinkling
Through the air
Ever so gently,
Roaming among the
Flowers,
Landing lightly on
Your shoulder.

## Reading Connections

This poem lends itself to an introduction of visualization. Although students can usually tell you how important it is to make pictures in their mind as they are reading text, they often struggle to do so. Giving students an opportunity to draw the images they are seeing in their heads while a fluent reader reads aloud to them helps them practice this important strategy. Poems usually have a narrow focus, but the word choices engage the imagination. To introduce "Butterfly," you might give students a piece of drawing paper divided in half. Let them know they will make two drawings as you read a poem to them. Their first drawing will be like a rough draft—their first attempt to capture the images evoked by the poet's words as the teacher reads. Ask your students to imagine the scene that the poem describes (be careful not to use the title or show the words—that comes later!). Then give them the opportunity to draw it. Don't be surprised if some students hear a word like "twinkling" and draw a picture of stars. After they finish have them share their drawings with a partner and talk about similarities and differences. Then read the poem aloud a second time. Students can use the ideas of their classmates as well as their own from the second read to revise their drawings.

After students share their revised drawings (we hope most will have a butterfly), ask them to explain what words in the poem helped them infer what the poet was describing. They may need to hear the poem again in order to remember exact words and phrases. Write these on the board and ask the students to use them to create labels for their revised drawing. What words or phrases helped them make an inference? Ask your students to explain their thinking aloud.

Rose was working with a group of second graders who, at first, were very puzzled by the poem "Butterfly." After hearing it read aloud several times, some still had difficulty anchoring the images in their mind. Most drew separate images linked to the words—bobbing for apples, stars, flowers in a garden. Logan, however, drew a large butterfly for his first drawing (Figure 4.5). When Rose asked him to explain his thinking he responded that "flowers" made him think of a garden. Since stars are usually not in a garden he thought about how the sun might make a butterfly's wings twinkle. He then decided that when butterflies move they mostly go up and down like bobbing. The other second graders in the group were amazed at this thinking and agreed that Logan was indeed on to something. They all incorporated his ideas into their own as they revised their drawings. Jessica began to repeat the stars in her second drawing, but later replaced them with the sun (Figure 4.6). "You see butterflies and flowers in the day," she explained. "Stars twinkle at night, so it must be the butterflies that are twinkling."

Rose explained to the students that this is exactly what readers do as they move through text—they revise their thinking based on new information and new ideas shared through discussion. They make inferences and create new images that lead to a deeper understanding. One of the benefits of this lesson is the opportunity to collect a formative assessment from

**Figure 4.5** Logan's drawings in response to "Butterfly"

**Figure 4.6** Jessica responds to "Butterfly."

each child. From the drawings, Rose was able to determine which students could revise prior thinking based on the thinking of others and multiple reads of the poem.

As a final step in this lesson, display the poem in some way so that the students can read the poem silently and aloud. Most likely, one or several of your students will quickly discover that the beginning letters of each line spell out the word "butterfly." Here is an opportunity to discuss acrostic poems if you have not already done so.

"Butterfly" is a great poem to show students how punctuation plays a major role in fluency and its link with comprehension. The poem is divided into four chunks, using a semicolon, commas, and a period. As you model what it means to read this poem fluently, your students will notice that you are not pausing or stopping until you get to a punctuation mark. Readers, especially struggling readers, often pause or stop at the end of a line even though it is not a complete thought. This poem will help students understand how phrasing works. They can practice reading the poem as a choral read, echo read, and cloze read. A poem is a better way to practice proper phrasing because it doesn't have as many words as a paragraph or a page of narrative or informational text. Its simplicity will help students concentrate on proper phrasing and expression instead of being overwhelmed by words and decoding issues. You may want to follow up this lesson by rewriting the poem in paragraph form so that students can practice again not stopping at the end of a line and using the punctuation as a signal for pauses and full stops.

The strong verbs used in "Butterfly" offer opportunities for vocabulary investigations. By taking a word like "bobbing" you can create many graphic organizers to help students explore its meaning. One way to do a word picture is to place the word in the center of the page and brainstorm examples that would help demonstrate its meaning. For "bobbing" one fourth-grade class came up with these examples: apples in a tub of water at a Halloween party, buoys in the ocean, lures on a fishing line, heads keeping time to music, and bobble-head toys. Place these examples in picture and/or word form around the word you are investigating. For older students, ask them to use thesauruses or dictionaries to find possible synonyms or antonyms. They can also explore meaning variations of the root word (*bob*: a kind of haircut). In addition, students can write their own definition of the word and use it in an original sentence.

## Writing Connections

"Butterfly" makes use of strong verbs that organize the text into four chunks (see the Your Turn Lesson at the end of the chapter). Here is a chance to talk about the use of unusual verbs such as "bobbing" and ordinary or more common verbs such as "twinkling." In this poem the more ordinary verb is extraordinary because it is linked with a butterfly, not a star or the twinkling of an eye. Discuss the word choice with your students. Why did the poet choose that verb over others? How could a butterfly be like a star in the garden? This type of discussion can deepen students' thinking about words. You can ask students to begin to collect words from their personal reading that are used in new or unusual ways and that might find a way into their own writing.

The alliteration in the poem gives you the chance to talk about letter sounds and how they help to create an image. "Landing lightly" is great alliteration for a poem about a butterfly because the "l" is a soft sound. In this poem there is a splash of alliteration—just enough to perk up your ear—strategically placed as the last thought.

The poets use many prepositional phrases in this poem to build content and to help us place the butterfly in a setting. "Through the air," "among the flowers," and "on your shoulder" all answer the question where. Students can return to their own creations or previous notebook entries, narratives, or other works to try to add important content with prepositional phrases. While prepositional phrases answer the question where (and sometimes when), adverbs ending in "-ly" often answer the question how. If your students are unfamiliar with adverbs, this is a perfect time to introduce them to your students.

Embedding the teaching of grammar in writing workshop on a daily basis will help students learn how sentences work and how powerful words can be. The adverbs in this poem are movable. Practice rewriting the poem by placing the adverbs in a different spot. For example, the last line may read, "landing on your shoulder lightly" or "lightly landing on your shoulder."

❖    ❖    ❖    ❖    ❖

### Jewel
*by Steven Schnur*

Just as the
Evening lights come on,
White flakes begin falling
Earthward, glittering
Like diamonds.

## Reading Connections

This poem provides an opportunity to explore phonics using an inquiry approach. Students can hunt for words that are spelled using the short and long "i" vowel sounds, chart and then sort them. They may discover some familiar patterns and some new patterns as well. Students can discuss their findings and come up with theories as to why certain combinations of letters produce specific sounds. When children are able to discover patterns, they are likely to use more efficient decoding skills and develop better spelling habits. Students can continue to find words in their independent reading and create charts of word families. You might also use this poem to investigate or reinforce blends ("fl," "gl").

In order to have a deep understanding of what looks like a simple poem at first glance, students can discuss the title of the poem, "Jewel," and what it tells you about the author's point of view. The simile within the poem compares snowflakes to glittering diamonds. This simile reinforces the big idea—snowflakes are precious jewels. The title is a synthesis of the poet's thoughts expressed as a metaphor. Ask students to compare their perspective with the author's point of view. Would they also think of snowflakes as jewels?

Setting is also important in many poems as an element of story. You could ask your students to think about this poem as if it had been set in the daytime. The dramatic background of night certainly influenced the poet's thinking about snowflakes and how he described the snowfall. This poem is written in the present tense and gives us a sense of being in the moment, just as the action is happening. Students often overlook time as another important element of setting, noticing the where but not the when. Here is a chance to explore the when in a setting: winter, nighttime, now.

Within the same work, Schnur has another acrostic poem, "Flurry." Students can compare the two poems for similes and the images they evoke as well as the author's point of view. How are these poems the same and/or different? How do the illustrations support the text?

## Writing Connections

It is important for students to recognize how words can sometimes act as a different part of speech within the context of a sentence. Nouns can act as powerful adjectives and capture a picture in a single word. Students can look at the phrase "evening lights" and immediately recognize that "evening" is an adjective most often used as a noun. Ask students to brainstorm other possible phrases where a noun becomes an adjective. In one fourth-grade classroom students created this list: rainbow skies, diamond nights, summer nights, midnight eyes, sunshine faces, jungle songs, straw hair, jelly knees, wind tunnels, velvet fur, winter day. Encourage students to continue to list these super-adjectives (adjectives that can act as a noun) with the nouns they describe in their writer's notebooks.

Examine "Jewel" and count the number of sentences. Students may be surprised to find out that this acrostic is one complete thought. The punctuation helps the poet write down his thinking in this one-sentence-structure acrostic poem. In order to help your writers imitate this structure, ask them to write down their thoughts about a topic. Lynne chose "rain" and "rainy days" to work with a third- and fourth-grade classroom. First, the class brainstormed a list of words about rain, including how students felt about the rain, activities for rainy days, sounds and sights for rainy days, and even rainy-day apparel. Then Lynne asked them to use those words to express one or two complete thoughts. The young writers, working in pairs and guided by their teachers, produced many ideas. Here are some examples that were charted for all to use:

> Rain falls from the sky like musical notes and drenches the world in its song.
> You can hear the soft pitter-patter. Rain provides a drink to thirsty plants.
> Rain drums on the window panes and rooftops. Thunder and lightning join in to provide entertainment.
> Umbrellas open on drizzly days and rain boots delight in the puddles.

Working with their prose, Lynne and the teachers asked students to use "rain" as the acrostic structure, borrow ideas from the chart, and create a poem around a single thought. It is important that students understand they are free to revise the words or thoughts on the chart to fit their poem. These poems were created as shared writing experiences:

> **R**ain falls from the sky
> **A**nd gives a cool drink to thirsty plants
> **I**n the garden on this
> **N**ew-summer day.
>
> **R**ain boots splish
> **A**nd splash
> **I**n deep puddles and feet
> **N**ever get wet!

Rain rings on rooftops
And window panes
In sweet musical
Notes:
Silver bells
Of Mother
Nature's
Gardens.

❖    ❖    ❖    ❖    ❖

## Worldly Wise
### by Avis Harley

Comma-size
And worldly wise,
The tiny caterpillar arrives
Eager to feed on leafy green—
Ravenous, greedy feasting machine!
Plumping up until it splits to shed
Its skin for one that fits—
Lively stripes grow bold in rows as
Larger and larger the larva grows.
And then—it ends this gorging bliss,
Retiring as a chrysalis.

## Reading Connections

The rhyme schemes in this poem can be used with students of any age, even though the words, and perhaps the concepts, are sophisticated. Young students can listen for the rhyming words and have an opportunity to play with sound. Some of the rhyming couplets do not always appear as the final words in the line. Students will notice that the poet sometimes needed to change the position of rhyming words in order to complete a thought that spanned two lines or more.

In addition to phonological awareness, the rhyming pairs offer an opportunity to examine different spelling patterns for the same sounds. For example, look at "green" and "machine," "size" and "wise," and "bliss" and "chrysalis." Older students may notice that the poet's choice of "arrives" is an almost-rhyme for "size" and "wise." The poet often uses the same vowel sounds within a line to create a rhythm and a delight in language. Notice, for

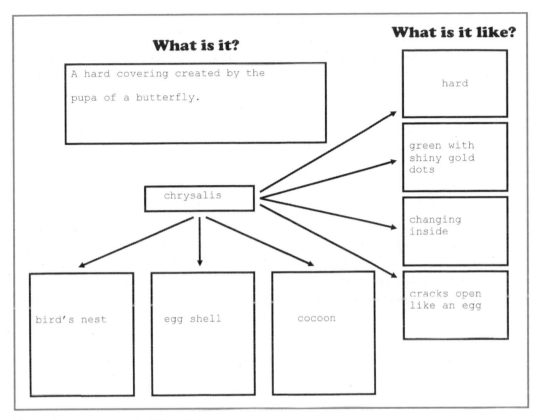

**What is it?**

A hard covering created by the pupa of a butterfly.

chrysalis

**What is it like?**

hard

green with shiny gold dots

changing inside

cracks open like an egg

bird's nest

egg shell

cocoon

**Figure 4.7** Concept map for "chrysalis"

example, the sound of long "e" in "eager to feed on leafy green" and the sound of short "u" in "plumping up until it splits to shed." By studying phonics elements in context, students are better able to transfer their knowledge of sounds as they read connected text.

The words in this poem give students a look at academic vocabulary that might be used in a science unit of study about life cycles. The adjective choices lend themselves to word study in the form of word maps. These adjectives are words that will appear in everyday content or pleasure reading. The nouns can be explored through concept of definition maps (see *Guided Comprehension: A Teaching Model for Grades 3–8* by Maureen McLaughlin and Mary Beth Allen [2002] and Figure 4.7 for an example).

Students will be able to interpret this poem more easily if they understand that it explains only a part of a life cycle and that events are placed in a certain order. The acrostic structure, CATERPILLAR, helps the reader know what part of the life cycle the poet is describing here. The title of the poem, "Worldly Wise," can lead to a rich discussion. What does it mean to be worldly wise and how can a caterpillar be described this way?

It is interesting to note that there are other acrostic poems in Harley's book that complete the life cycle of a monarch butterfly. These include "Monarch Beginnings," "Getting Ready," and "Final Finery." It would be interesting to read all four poems to see the whole life cycle in a new way and compare and contrast the information gleaned from reading the poems to the information gathered from a textbook or other nonfiction book about butterflies. Ask students to evaluate the form of delivering the information. Which did they like best, the poetry or prose, and why?

## Writing Connections

Word choice is important to poets because a poem's format is fairly short as compared to a story or article. "Worldly Wise" is full of vibrant adjectives and precise nouns. You can begin a discussion by talking about the use of alliteration in this poem such as "larger and larger the larva grows" and its effectiveness in the title, "Worldly Wise." Encourage students to find other titles in poems, books, and newspaper headlines that make use of alliteration and discuss why it is effective. Note the use of the hyphenated adjective "comma-size" as a sit-up-and-take-notice lead into the poem. Students can create synonym and antonym word wheels for wonderful adjectives such as "ravenous" (Figure 4.8), "greedy" (Figure 4.9), and "lively." In one sixth-grade classroom the students partnered to examine "ravenous" and "greedy."

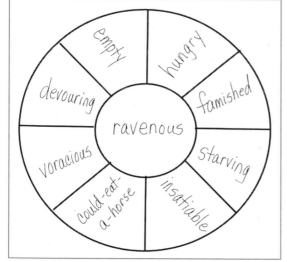

**Figure 4.8** Word wheel for "ravenous"

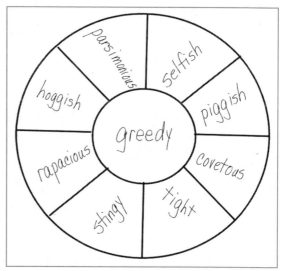

**Figure 4.9** Word wheel for "greedy"

Older students can appreciate the juxtaposition of what would commonly be referred to as "green leaves" to "leafy green." Ask students which phrase sounds more like poetry and why they think so. Note the use of the word "gorging" as an adjective to describe "bliss." Calling attention to this unexpected word choice can help students be more cognizant of the words they select for their own poems and stories.

Many student poems are written without the use of punctuation marks. The poetry of Avis Harley will serve as rich models for studying convention use in poems. It is a common practice for students to overuse the exclamation mark. A discussion about the one exclamatory sentence the poet uses and its position in the poem may help students rethink their frequent use of this punctuation mark. You can lead students to an understanding that exclamation marks cannot be used as periods. In this poem, the exclamation mark accentuates the main idea. You can also call attention to the poet's use of dashes. The first dash is used to signal that an important idea is coming. The second dash is used to connect two ideas, the second idea being a restatement of the first. The final dash is used as a dramatic pause to communicate a change to the reader. After students investigate and theorize about the use of dashes and exclamation marks, they can try it out in their own writing. Or, they can look at a previously written piece and revise accordingly.

❖   ❖   ❖   ❖   ❖

### Drawing
**by Judy Young**

Delightful pictures
Released onto paper
As
Wild
Imaginations are
Netted with the
Grasp of a crayon.

## Reading Connections

This poem immediately lends itself to a lesson in making text connections. The information Young presents in a sidebar format in her book *R Is for Rhyme: A Poetry Alphabet* will help students understand the illustrator's rendition of this poem. We learn that Lewis Carroll included an acrostic in *Through the Looking Glass*, and that the illustrator drew a picture of Carroll watching Alice draw picture after picture of characters such as the Cheshire Cat, the Mad Hatter, and the White Rabbit. Certainly, Carroll's story is a wonderful example of wild imaginings that conjure up wonderful pictures in the reader's mind. When you read the acrostic with your students, ask them to think about other favorite books that conjure up wild imaginings and discuss the pictures that they see in their minds. This discussion can shift your focus to visualization of text and show how it helps us deepen comprehension.

Although the number of words used in this poem is small, they are well chosen, and a discussion around them can lead your students to make inferences they might not have noticed on an initial read. For example, examining the words "netted," "released," and "wild" will help your students understand the implied metaphor that the poet presents. It's as if she wants us to think that the wild imaginations held captive in our brains are alive. When we draw, we open the gates to our imaginings, allowing them to spill out onto paper. The word "crayon" may help the reader infer that the poet wants us to imagine the artist of these drawings as a young child. These words can also be used to build vocabulary by exploring possible synonyms and antonyms.

## Writing Connections

Word choice is an important part of creating the author's voice, or writing style. The writer carefully chooses his words to carry his ideas. The word study begun after reading the poem can continue in the writing workshop. Students can find the key verbs in the poem and talk about why the poet chose them over other verbs. How are they related to extend the metaphor? Why does the poet choose to write them in the passive voice?

You and your students can use the poem as a scaffold to find other words that would still maintain the acrostic structure. Students can partner and work with thesauruses and dictionaries to find other choices. For example, "dreamy," "daring," and delicious" could also describe "pictures" yet maintain the structure. "Paintings," "portraits," and "sketches" could be substituted for "pictures." What instruments other than crayons could be used to create pictures? Substitutions for "wild" could include "wondrous," "winning," "wide," and "whimsical." Here is an example using word substitutions for this poem from Lynne's notebook:

Daring sketches
Riding across the paper
As
Wondrous
Imaginations are
Nipped from within,
Growing real with the help of a pencil.

Ponder this question with students: Were certain words chosen over others because the letters of the acrostic controlled the word choice?

❖    ❖    ❖    ❖    ❖

## Sipping the Sunset
### by Avis Harley

Rooting around
In the Zambezi—river life looks
Very easy, slurping down an
Evening drink, then
Rolling in luscious mud to sink

Right into delicious squish—what more could
Ever a hippo wish? Faithful birds
Vacuum the hide and
Efficient fish clean teeth inside.
Rich is the life that lazes
In sun, *but* . . . if
Ever you see a hippo run—RUN!

## Reading Connections

The rhymes in this poem are sophisticated. Reading the poem aloud, your students will hear them, but they will not necessarily find them as easily with their eyes. The acrostic form places them internally, and occasionally rhymes a word within one line with a word that ends the next line. Look for these rhyming pairs: "Zambezi" and "easy," "drink" and "sink," "squish" and "wish," "hide" and "inside," "sun" and "run." Students discover that the acrostic scaffold led the poet to this organizational rhyme scheme in order to sustain complete thought units while still conveying the delight of rhyme.

This poem is also great for practicing fluency. Students can notice the many different forms of punctuation used, as well as the variation in print, and figure out what they signal to the reader. Students can discuss and interpret how to read the commentary dash and the ellipses as they practice reading different kinds of sentences—declarative, interrogative, and exclamatory.

This poem links easily to its content area. Your readers will be able to clearly see how a poet can convey information (the symbiotic relationship between hippos, birds, and fish) through an acrostic form. Poetry can give us an efferent as well as an aesthetic experience.

Even though the title is "Sipping the Sunset," the acrostic structure spells out "river reverie." This gives your students an opportunity to discuss the synthesis of ideas. How is the title related to the words used for the acrostic?

Everyday words like "rooting" and "rich" can be examined for multiple meanings. Some of the words in this poem also lend themselves to studying point of view. Pairing words like "delicious" with "squish" and "luscious" with "mud" helps the reader think like a hippo.

Understanding organizational structure will help readers deepen their comprehension. In this poem, the transition word "but" paired with the ellipses signals a change in the tone and structure of the poem. Everything up to this point was description. Now the poet is offering advice. The reader will appreciate the sharp (and unexpected) transition of a mild-mannered hippo lazing in the water into a dangerous beast.

## Writing Connections

This poem offers many mentor sentences to expand your writers' possibilities for using more varied sentence structures. Ask them to examine the sentence "Rich is the life that lazes in sun." Students from one fifth-grade class came up with these imitations in a shared writing experience, which were listed on an anchor chart:

> Content is the puppy that naps in a lap.
> Cruel is the winter that blasts us with blizzards.
> Wise is the student that learns his lesson.
> Beautiful is the night that is bathed in starlight.

To extend this study, ask students to create more of their own sentences in their writer's notebooks and share them with a response group or with the class. Choose one of the sentences and model how you could use it as the first line in a poem, the lead sentence in an essay, or the lead-in to a narrative. Another option is to revise previously written work by changing a sentence into this structure or adding a sentence that uses this structure. This particular sentence structure also lends itself to being the conclusion or final thought in a poem, story, or informational text. It helps students express their point in a unique way.

Students might also study the structure in this sentence: "Rooting around in the Zambezi—river life looks very easy." Writers can note how these sentence parts can be interchangeable (River life looks very easy—rooting around in the Zambezi.) Challenge them to create other sentences with interchangeable parts.

## Your Turn Lesson

# WRITING AN ACROSTIC POEM AROUND STRONG VERBS

Most teachers would agree that vocabulary lessons are best remembered when they are embedded in a reading or writing lesson rather than studied in isolation. This lesson is a way to help students expand their vocabulary and knowledge of parts of speech in a meaningful way, and it easily lends itself to work with a thesaurus or dictionary. By connecting it to research in a content area, you can provide your students with an additional, interesting way to demonstrate what they have learned.

**Hook:** Return to the poem "Butterfly" in *Silver Seeds*. As students read it again, ask them to pay close attention to the verbs the poet uses. Discuss the importance of precise verbs giving the reader a clear picture. Examine other poems in *Silver Seeds*, such as "Hummingbird," "Sun," and "Leaf," which make use of precise verbs.

**Purpose:** *Writers, today I'm going to show you how you can focus on verbs to help you write an acrostic poem.*

**Brainstorm:** Just about any topic can be used as a starting point in this lesson, but it should be something students have some knowledge of. Since this writing activity lends itself to cross-curricular connections, you might want to use topics your students are studying in science or social studies. For example, a unit on zoo animals might yield the following list: monkeys, elephants, bears, giraffes, zebras, pandas, lions, tigers, hippos, and rhinos.

**Model:** Choose an animal from the list and write a short paragraph about that animal that contains some interesting facts. If necessary, show students how you might check information or do some quick research using a book, article, or Internet site. Here's a sample paragraph about a hippopotamus compiled from a variety of sources including *African Acrostics: A Word in Edgeways* by Avis Harley:

> Hippos are heavy, large mammals that live in rivers or lakes. They love to wallow in mud to keep cool. Hippos are territorial. One male rules over a certain stretch of river and the females and young that live there. Hippos use their strong legs to walk or run along the bottom of the river. They leave the river at dusk to graze on short grasses.

The next step would be to underline or list the verbs used in the paragraph and to think of synonyms (perhaps with the help of a thesaurus) that might fit with the letters needed for an acrostic about the animal. In this example, you would probably call attention to the verbs "wallow," "live," "rules," "use," "walk," "run," "leave," and "graze." Although "wallow" is a great verb, it doesn't fit easily in an acrostic using "hippo," but other words that suggest its meaning do. You could also brainstorm related verbs that are suggested by the facts in the paragraph. The more words you have to work with, the better. Finally, work with the verbs and ideas to compose your poem.

**H**anging around
**I**n the mud,
**P**residing over a river domain,
**P**ulling out to graze
**O**n grasses.

**Shared/Guided Writing:** Choose another subject from your list and follow the same procedure with help from your students. Alternately, students can work in partnerships or triads to create an acrostic poem emphasizing verbs.

**Independent Writing:** Invite students to create their own acrostic poems using ideas from the brainstormed list. Or, they can try a new acrostic with verbs as the focus on a different topic, perhaps something suggested from their territories or expert lists in their writer's notebooks.

**Reflection:** Ask students to reflect on how the activity worked for them.

*How did focusing on verbs help you write your acrostic poem?*
*Was it difficult to find verbs to fit the letters you were using?*
*What resources did you find to be most helpful? When could you use them again?*

## Your Turn Lesson

### WRITING ACROSTICS AROUND NOUNS THAT NAME SOMEONE WHO . . .

Linking word study with writing will help students make reading-writing connections and learn more about word structures at the same time. Using a common suffix such as "-er" presents an interesting way to create an acrostic poem and review the suffix and its purpose, all within one lesson.

**Hook:** Return to the book *Summer: An Alphabet Acrostic* by Steven Schnur and his poem "Jogger." As you and your students read the poem several times, notice how this acrostic is built around what the jogger is doing and how he is feeling about it. Students can examine the acrostic word, talk about the root word, and note how the spelling changes when the suffix is added to the word. Ask students to think about a time when they were joggers or they saw other people jogging. Where were they? Why do people jog? What might you see where you jog?

**Purpose:** *Writers, today I'm going to show you how to use a noun to write an acrostic poem.*

**Brainstorm:** Review with your students how the "-er" suffix changes the part of speech and the meaning of the base word. Write several verbs on a chart or whiteboard and show their "-er" form. For example:

farm  ⟶  farmer
paint  ⟶  painter

Ask students to brainstorm other examples in their notebooks with a partner using this same scaffold. Create an anchor chart of the nouns that use the "-er" suffix. Some additional nouns could include: writer, builder, player, teacher, preacher, researcher, babysitter, gardener, singer, dancer, pitcher, runner, winner. (Note: some nouns such as sailor, conductor, sculptor, and governor may require the "-or" suffix.)

**Model:** After choosing a word from the brainstormed chart, use chart paper to think aloud while you record your thoughts about where the person is, what he is doing, and how he feels about it. Don't worry about the acrostic form at this point—you are simply gathering as many ideas as you can so you have a pool to choose from. Here are some examples from Lynne's notebook for "writer":

trying to find the right words
wonderful words in perfect places
brainstorm, list, or draw a picture
notice things about their world
sitting in front of a computer
wondering
staring out the window
resources: pencils, pens, paper, notebooks
sometimes words spill easily
painting a picture with words
sometimes it's hard to get started
always think of your target audience
make it seem real even if it's fantasy
revise often
don't forget the final edit

For younger students, model drawing a picture and labeling it. Then write the word you are using in the acrostic format and think aloud as you use your ideas to compose your poem:

Wondering what is happening
Right outside my window,
I suddenly spy a single leaf
Trying not to fall, so I
Eke out the picture into my notebook.
Revision will come later.

Notice how Lynne describes the setting. You can even infer the time of year (reading connection). Next she describes what she is doing and lets the reader in on her writing process (she revises after all her thoughts are down on paper.) As you write, you may notice that you use some ideas that weren't on your list, or you may need to find a synonym for a word as Lynne does with "eke" instead of "paint." Make sure to point this out to your students; sometimes they think they can only use words or ideas that were brainstormed.

**Shared/Guided Writing:** Choose another word from the list and do the same thing together as a group. Or place students in small groups or partnerships to create a collaborative poem. One group of fifth graders composed "Painter" from a list of their collective thinking:

> **P**lacing color
> **A**cross a canvas,
> **I**nviting
> **N**ew eyes
> **T**o linger over and
> **E**njoy the
> **R**ealistic scene.

**Independent Writing:** Invite students to return to the brainstormed list and add other possibilities in their writer's notebook before drafting a poem around a single word. For instance, a student who has a pet cat may suddenly think of the word *hunter* because she has a picture in her head of her cat bringing her a mouse as a gift. Another student may think of the last baseball game he played where he hit a double and think of *hitter*. Don't be concerned that your students are spending a lot of time brainstorming and creating lists and drawings in their notebooks. Here is a perfect time to give students the opportunity to practice using thesauruses, dictionaries, content-area books, electronic sources, and picture files. These snapshots become a permanent source of ideas and can be used to build content in other types of writing.

**Reflection:** Ask students to reflect on how the lesson worked for them.

> *How did creating the words help them better understand what a suffix does?*
> *How did their notes help them to write an acrostic poem?*
> *Was it easy or difficult to work within the acrostic structure? Why?*

# CHAPTER 5

# The Persona Poem:
# Writing in the Voice of Another

### railroad tracks
*by Ralph Fletcher*

I got built ninety years back by
sweating stinking swearing men.

For decades every kind of train
screeched on my back. No more.

Winters here can be pretty bleak
but wildflowers always come back.

Empty nests have that forlorn look
'til the songbirds return in May.

The swamp is quiet but soon frogs
will take up their monotonous chant.

My back remains unbroken but only
ghost locomotives rattle these rails.

Writing a persona poem is a powerful experience for students. They can temporarily become another person, an animal, a pet, an object, a character from a book, or even a body part or article of clothing. You can write in the voice of a person who has an unusual occupation such as a window cleaner for skyscrapers, an archeologist, or an astronaut. Persona poetry gives students a chance to think outside the box and ride the winds of their imaginations as Shria, a fourth grader, did when she imagined herself as the moon:

### The Moon

I am the moon.
I like to relax.
I am shiny and bright.
I am a slow and sneaky spy.
I often lose parts because of the weight of meteorites.
I sometimes get visitors from planet Earth.
I feel lonely and empty.
I am the moon.

Looking at persona poems will give young writers from kindergarten through high school a chance to try out an idea that may otherwise seem too fantastical or out of the ordinary to accept or write about. This style of poetry is heavily influenced by fiction and fantasy. The writer must leave behind his point of view and take on another. The sky is the limit! As a writer you are given a free pass to undergo metamorphosis and change your style and point of view, at least for the length of one poem.

Wearing different masks, our student-writers can safely reveal their feelings about a social or personal issue by looking at it from the other side. In *Nonfiction Craft Lessons: Teaching Informational Writing K–8*, JoAnn Portalupi and Ralph Fletcher (2001) refer to this kind of writing as writing through a mask. Writers can temporarily adopt another voice and try it on for size. That voice can suit how they are feeling at that moment in writing workshop. If, for example, they are feeling lonely, they might write in the voice of their school during summer vacation when it is empty of children and teachers.

Sometimes persona poetry takes on a special format. In *Butterfly Eyes and Other Secrets of the Meadow*, poet Joyce Sidman creates persona poetry using a friendly-letter format in "Letter to the Sun" and "Letter to the Rain." Other times the poet addresses her audience in the voice of her subject matter such as a milkweed plant in "Heavenly."

Sometimes students find it easier to write a persona poem as an extended metaphor or through the use of personification. In other words, the poem is written by another who perceives the object as a living thing. You will notice that we have chosen both types of poems to explore in this chapter. Students could choose to write their poems in the third person and later revise by using first-person voice (writing in the persona of someone or something else). Or students can write from their own perspective (in their own voice) and directly speak to an animal, biome, book character, or object.

In order to help your students get started, you could bring in some concrete objects to display in your poetry corner. Collect things you think your students might find interesting. Of course, these objects could vary according to the age of your students. They can include collectibles such as a snow globe, a charm bracelet, or a special hat. Kitchen objects like a whisk, a spoon, or a rolling pin could get writing started. Another option is to ask your students to bring in something they could write about in the voice of that object.

In Frank Murphy's fifth-grade classroom, students wrote different kinds of persona poems. Many students chose a familiar object from home or the classroom. Victoria speaks in the voice of her hairbrush, creating a picture in our mind of the journey of a hairbrush:

> I am a tool,
> being worked on to be made
> perfect,
> in the huge factory.
> A girl picks me up and takes me home with her.
> I see brunette and strips of gold
> as the girl holds me,
> and moves me.
> I feel myself bump, bump, bumping,
> like a roller-coaster.
> I am persistent,
> keep pushing and pushing,
> until my path is clear
> and now easy to go through and straight,
> until the next morning after a long sleep,
> the girl grabs me again
> and that cycle continues,
> once again.
> I am a hair brush.

Once Natalie, another fifth grader from Frank's class, got started writing persona poems she couldn't stop! Natalie wrote about a book (see Chapter 7), February 29, and a keyboard. She even wrote in the persona of an emotion, hatred. Here's her persona poem written in the voice of a keyboard:

I can spell any words
and
know all punctuations
I wince when people hit,
hit my keys
and
when they spell a word
wrong
most houses have me
and authors use
me a lot
I save you from using a pencil
I am a keyboard

The students were so excited about writing persona poems that Frank extended this writing into his work with current events. At this particular time there were many news stories about tornado disasters. Notice Gabriella's use of strong verbs and short sentences that help us visualize the funnel:

I rip
I twist
I spin
I tear
I am big
I am grey
I pick things up
And destroy them
I make a mess
I am a tornado

Lynne and fourth-grade teacher Karen Drew transitioned into their work with persona poetry by using Joyce Sidman's *This Is Just to Say: Poems of Apology and Forgiveness* inspired by "This Is Just to Say," a poem by William Carlos Williams. Lynne wrote an apology poem about the time she borrowed her sister's beautiful white sweater, new and with the tags still attached, without asking for permission. Karen took a different twist and decided to write in the voice of the wicked stepmother in the Cinderella fairy tale. Other options could include writing apology poems in the voice of the candlestick from the familiar nursery rhyme "Jack Be Nimble" or in the voice of the lamb from "Mary Had a Little Lamb." For some of your students, it will be a chance to hear nursery rhymes for the first time! Explore nursery rhymes to create apology persona poems with your students. Here is Karen's model for her fourth graders:

> This is just to say
>
> I have thwarted your
> Chances of
> "Happily Ever After"
>
> That you were
> Hoping to find
> At the royal ball
>
> Forgive me,
> The house is just
> So dirty, so dingy and
> So in need of cleaning

For older students, read *If the Shoe Fits: Voices from Cinderella* by Laura Whipple. Her poems include the voices of characters and objects from this familiar fairy tale.

Karen's students brainstormed a list of possible voices for apology poems. The fourth graders listed only voices they felt they could write in without doing further reading or research. Sarah wrote in the voice of her pet rabbit:

> This is just to say
> I have nibbled all of your carrots
> In the purple bowl . . .
> which you were probably
> saving for a snack . . .
> Forgive me,
> my cage was left open
> and the carrots were just so
> crispy-irresistible!

Amelia wrote a similar poem in the voice of her dog, but held off until the end to let the reader know for sure who is speaking in her poem. The element of surprise made this poem a big hit among her peers:

This is just to say
I have hungrily gobbled the pie on the counter
That you were probably saving
For your Thanksgiving feast.
Forgive me.
It was overwhelmingly delicious . . .
Such a sugary crust,
What a splendid apple cinnamon taste,
So delicious I barked in satisfaction:
Ruff! Ruff!

(See the Your Turn Lesson at the end of this chapter for more ideas on writing persona apology poems.)

Then Karen and Lynne shared *I Didn't Do It* by Patricia MacLachlan and Emily MacLachlan Charest, a book of poems written in the voice of puppies. Some students chose to write a question poem in the voice of their pet, addressing their human owner. Others, like Tyler, imitated the poem "Rules." Tyler wrote about what he knew best: cats.

## Cat Rules

Your Rules:
Don't scratch
Don't play with yarn
Take a bath every day
Don't hiss
Don't drink milk
Don't cough fur balls
Don't lie on my lap

I don't like your rules!

My Rules:
Lie on human laps
Pet me every chance you get
Play with yarn
Drink milk every day forever
Never ever take baths
Eat fish with a side of mice for dinner.

I love my rules!

It's always rewarding when students transfer their learning to new situations. In one third-grade class, the teacher, Joanne Costello, asked her students to summarize their thinking after a science unit on light. One of the students, Emily, asked if she could express her thinking in the form of a poem. Joanne was surprised with Emily's persona poem written in the voice of a shadow:

### Silhouette

I am as dark as night
Calm as an ocean breeze
Identical in every way
But one
I have no color or face
I am a sister, twin, or brother
I am the same in every way
A friend to trust, to love, to share
I am a creation of Earth
I am magic
I am good
A true honest friend that comes and goes

Persona poetry is a wonderful way to write multigenre pieces. The poems can lead a reader into a research project about biomes, magnetism, or an era of history. By writing in the voices of world leaders, we can make history come alive and help students let other people's thinking in. Persona poems are also a good way to introduce point of view and author's purpose.

Of course, the main thing to remember about a persona poem is a change in point of view. You aren't just writing about another person, you are writing as if you *were* that other person. You try to think, feel, and act like that person, animal, object, or biome—or even something as abstract as a color or concept such as equality. Will Mowery's poem "A Slave to Grubby Hands" screams in the voice of an emotional pencil that laments his present condition and reminisces about his former state. Students can easily relate to this poem and will find its humor particularly appealing.

### A Slave to Grubby Hands

I'm a slave to a kid with grubby hands.
Yeah, I mean you.
You know I mean you.

Don't look at me like some kind of innocent little babe.

You're long past being innocent.

You're long past being a little babe.

What're you—like ten? twelve?

Innocent little babe? I don't think so.

I cannot believe the way you make me work.

You're wearing me out with all that chicken scratching you do.

If I was a hill, you'd be the wind and rain that washes me away.

I'm disappearing before my very eyes.

Going . . . Going . . . and soon I'll be gone.

I can remember when I was nice and long like a fat juicy spaghetti—

okay, maybe not juicy, but you get the idea—

But now! Now I'm like the size of your pinkie finger, for pete's sake!

You're killing me!

Scratch, scratch, scratch all day long. Sitting in that messy desk of yours.

Scratch, scratch, scratch, scratch, scratch, scratch, scratch—like a grubby chicken.

And I haven't even mentioned what you're doing to my head.

If you can even call it a head anymore.

My head. Oh, such a beautiful head—long and round and pink—such a soft, supple pink.

Now. It's almost gone.

It's a wonder I can even think, it's so far gone.

The way you keep abusing it scratching off that chicken scratching of yours is a crime.

You're killing me from both ends!

Those are my brains and guts you're spilling out onto that piece of paper of yours.

And you tell me all that scratching says something.

I don't hear it saying anything.

Silence! That's what I hear.

Nothing!

Zilch!

Zippo!

Zero!

Nada!

Nothing! Nothing! Nothing!

# CLASSROOM CONNECTIONS: THE PERSONA POEM

## Empire State Building
### *by J. Patrick Lewis*

I am an American boy, standing up to the world.
I sleep, the city sleeps. We dream
    the riveter's dream, held island-fast.
I wake to taxi alarms.
I am a 102-stop elevator ride to heaven.
I am ten million bricks of unshakable faith.
I capture imagination at its peak.
I hugged King Kong, he hugged me back.
I look down Broadway for a work of art,
    the Fulton Fish Market for a slice of life,
    United Nations Headquarters for a little peace.
It's lonely up here without my big twin brothers,
    the World Trade Center Towers.
Wait here on my doorstep, Central Park,
    while I look over Harlem.
I am an American boy, face to face with the world.

## Reading Connections

"Empire State Building" is a wonderful poem to show students the importance of activating prior knowledge before the first read and during the first read. Students who are familiar with New York City may begin to make connections and form pictures in their minds. Students who have never visited Manhattan or the famous monument will have to rely on what they have read or seen in movies, books, magazines, television, and newspapers. You can search for a video clip for background on King Kong or fill in the gaps by reading a picture book like *Sky Boys: How They Built the Empire State Building* by Deborah Hopkinson. You can also help your students make cross-curricular connections in geography, history, and even mathematics. In particular, students will need a partial understanding of the Great Depression in order to appreciate the symbolic nature of this monument. Additional reading can be accomplished in small groups or with a partner to find out more about the places the poet mentions including the Fulton Fish Market, the United Nations Headquarters, the World Trade Center Towers, and Harlem.

Another way to activate background knowledge would be to use a K-W-L chart. Form small groups and ask students to brainstorm what they know about the Empire State Building and New York City. Ask the students to reach consensus before sharing. Any items they are unsure of should not be shared in whole group at this time. Chart information from all groups and use it as an informal assessment to figure out what they still need to know in order to comprehend this poem on a deeper level. Provide this knowledge in an appropriate format. For example, you may show your own photos of New York or find photographs, video clips, or articles on the Internet. Now is the time to allow students to pose questions or write about their wonderings in their reader response journal. These questions may generate new thinking and open the door for new questions as they read the poem.

"Empire State Building" is a poem that begs readers to make inferences. Once the prior knowledge has been established, you can easily create lessons that teach students what they need to do in order to infer. For example, after students have read about the Fulton Fish Market, they can infer that a "slice of life" simply refers to the daily hustle and bustle of shoppers from diverse backgrounds that frequent the market. Students can use their own understandings about "heaven" and the knowledge from the poem that the building is 102 stories to the observation deck to infer that it's extremely high.

This poem also serves as a vehicle for teaching symbolism. The Empire State Building was the first of its kind, constructed in a time of despair. It symbolized hope and, as the poet tells us, "unshakable faith" and "imagination at its peak." The poet clearly sees this monument as a symbol for America, beginning and ending his poem with "I am an American boy . . . ." He captures the youthful spirit of our country with the word "boy" and reminds us that even though the Empire State Building is old to many of us, it is relatively young compared to monuments in other countries around the world.

## Writing Connections

Perhaps one of the most beneficial uses of this poem in the writing workshop would be to study the poet's choice of words. Proper nouns help writers speak with the voice of authority. The proper nouns in this poem are purposeful and varied. The reader conjures up fantastical images of King Kong climbing the skyscraper and busy Broadway with flashing marquees. For those who remember, images of the World Trade Center Towers fill our minds with what was before and what happened on that tragic day. From proper noun to proper noun we get the feeling of bigness, of greatness. The building and the city in which it dwells inspire us. Remove the proper nouns from the poem and we remove the specificity that captures both pictures and feelings in our minds and hearts. Using this poem as a mentor text can help students understand the importance of using proper nouns, whenever they can, in all of their writing.

Many of the verbs used in this poem are written in the present tense to show that the actions are continuing over time. If you look carefully at the word choice you will notice that the poet uses opposites such as "wake" and "sleep," "big" and "little," and even "Central Park" and "Harlem."

This persona poem comes alive through its appeal to the senses and emotions. We hear the horns of the taxis, we feel the strength of its ten million bricks, we see the stars that are almost in our reach as we scrape the sky, we smell the fish from the marketplace, and we experience the loneliness after the demise of its "big twin brothers." In persona poetry it's important to use as many senses as naturally fit into the writing. This will help you to "walk around" in the skin of someone or something else.

J. Patrick Lewis brought this building to life in other ways, including the order of events within a line. For example, he allowed the Empire State Building to speak of hugging King Kong before the giant gorilla hugged him back. Of course, the use of first person perspective with pronouns such as "I," "we," and "me" help the reader imagine the Empire State Building as a living form.

You can also use this poem to study the use of punctuation in free-verse poetry. Once students understand how and why an author is punctuating his poem, they can use his techniques in their own writing. In "Empire State Building," J. Patrick Lewis uses commas in many different ways. You can discuss with your students why he chose a comma instead of a semicolon or a period in lines such as "I sleep, the city sleeps" or "I hugged King Kong, he hugged me back."

❖   ❖   ❖   ❖   ❖

### The Garden Hose
*by Beatrice Janosco*

In the gray evening
I see a long green serpent
With its tail in the dahlias.

It lies in loops across the grass
And drinks softly at the faucet.

I can hear it swallow.

## Reading Connections

We love the simplicity of this poem and its description of an everyday object in an interesting and unique form using persona poetry. The poet brings a garden hose to life, and the reader must read between the lines making inferences along the way. Close attention to setting reveals not only where but when, so often overlooked by students in our classrooms. We can infer that it is dusk when we read "in the gray evening" and that we are outside in a summer garden with the mention of "dahlias." If students are unfamiliar with dahlias, provide some time to explore resources on the Internet or in the library that can help them build background knowledge. This work will allow students to visualize the poet's small moment in time. While they are searching, you could ask them to find two or three other names of flowers they are unfamiliar with and write a short description in their reader response journal or vocabulary journal.

Metaphor is a difficult literary device for students to understand when they come across it in prose or poetry. In order to help students with metaphor, read this poem the first time and even the second time without providing the title. Ask the students to find the metaphor by citing clues that will help them understand that Janosco is not actually talking about a garden snake, but a garden hose. If your students are experiencing difficulty, ask this question: How can a garden hose be like a snake? As they compare these two things they will notice that both are found in a garden and both can be long and green, and so on. Make sure students understand that these are the kinds of questions they can ask themselves when trying to comprehend literature.

The ability to see similarities and differences is a skill used across grade levels and content areas. It's harder for students to describe differences than it is to note similarities. Poems are a wonderful resource to help students develop this skill because they are short and you can easily find several written around the same topic. In *The Great Frog Race and Other Poems*, Kristine O'Connell George also has a poem titled "Garden Hose." Like Janosco's poem, it personifies the garden hose but does not compare it to an animal. Instead, her garden hose takes on the quality of a person wondering what it will be when it grows up as it dozes in the warm sun and dreams. Students can also evaluate these poems and offer opinions as to which one they like best and why.

Of course, "The Garden Hose" is great for developing fluency not only because it is short, but because students need to pay attention to the punctuation instead of the line break in order to know when to stop.

## Writing Connections

When students write stories and poems, the addition of color words is probably the easiest thing they can do to help readers visualize. In "The Garden Hose" Janosco uses "gray" and "green"—the simplicity of her word choice blending in with the simplicity and serenity of this garden snapshot.

The noun "serpent" may call up a different picture than "snake." Students can brainstorm other synonyms that could be used here. Writers should discuss why the poet chose one word over another, possibly replacing words and reading the poem again for rhythm and even mood. A precise noun such as "dahlias" helps the writer develop specificity.

In addition, here is an opportunity to cultivate vocabulary. Students can make lists of different flowers in their writer's notebooks and learn about new kinds of flowers, extend their research to learn about native plants and trees, and get a chance to use color words, shape words, and size words to describe each flower on their list.

Other literary devices, such as the alliteration in "lies in loops" or the repetition of words beginning with the "gr" blend—"green," "grass," and "gray"—catch the reader's attention and help students appreciate the author's creativity.

Here is a poem where you could discuss line breaks and white space. Why does the poet choose to add white space before the final line: "I can hear it swallow."

This persona poem helps the reader imagine the hose as a living thing, a garden snake. Janosco brings it to life by appealing to the senses—we can see this serpent hose in a garden setting and even hear what it is doing. Using other senses as well as sight can dramatically change the impact a piece of writing has.

After reading this poem with one third-grade class, Lynne asked the students to brainstorm everyday objects they thought they could write a persona poem about. She also shared "Broom" by Tony Johnston and "Washing Machine" by Bobbi Katz, both from *Dirty Laundry Pile: Poems in Different Voices* selected by Paul B. Janeszko. She urged them to think about objects in their classroom and in their homes. The list included *spoon, globe, desk, pencil sharpener, chair, television, telephone,* and *vacuum cleaner.* They chose vacuum cleaner for a shared experience. Lynne asked them to visualize the vacuum cleaner and asked questions such as "What do you see?" "What is it doing?" "What animal does it remind you of?" "What do you hear?" These questions seemed to fit with a vacuum cleaner and also with the mentor poem. Other objects and poems may evoke other questions. After recording all the answers on the whiteboard, the class composed the following shared poem:

## Vacuum Cleaner

In the center of the living room
I see a tall, purple monster
With a licorice-stick tail.
It rushes before me across the carpet
And slowly eats my cracker crumbs.
I can hear it roar.

❖   ❖   ❖   ❖   ❖

## Monkey Wrench
### by Kristine O'Connell George

He jeers at me with a strong-jawed grin,
Juts out his wide silver chin—
Cranks the nuts tighter.
Biting stubborn rusted bolts,
Tackling hitches, engines, bikes,
No job's too big for him.
After a long hard day, monkey wrench
hangs upside down on his hook
above Dad's workbench,
yawning.

## Reading Connections

Understanding sequence of events is a skill students need to practice and acquire throughout their elementary school years. This poem has a definite sequence. The poet describes the different jobs the monkey wrench does during the day as he is put to work. The transition phrase "after a long hard day" signals that the work of the day is over and a change will occur—the monkey wrench is ready to rest. In addition, the word "yawning" implies that he (the monkey wrench) is tired, which gives students a chance to use their inference skills.

You can dive into vocabulary work with "Monkey Wrench." Since the poem is built around a tool, the poet uses words that fit the subject matter such as "workbench," "nuts," "cranks," "bolts," "hitches." Explore the meaning of less common verbs such as "jeers," "juts," and "cranks." Students can find synonyms in thesauruses and dictionaries. Challenge them to find word systems in their independent reading and figure out how the nomenclature helps to convince the reader that the writer is an expert in her field. Students can also have fun by investigating other uses for the term *monkey wrench* when using its alternate definition (to cause disruption).

Lead students to recognize that pronouns can help them identify text written as a personification of someone or something else. The poet refers to the monkey wrench as "he," "his," and "him," instead of "it" or "its." The use of the words "grin" and "chin" are also clues that this is a persona poem.

As with most other poems, "Monkey Wrench" can be used by students to practice fluency. The different forms of punctuation at the ends of the lines in this poem vary: commas, dash, and period. Why did the poet choose one over the other? Which pause is longer, which harsher?

## Writing Connections

One way to get started writing a persona poem around an object is to think of words that are connected with the object and create a word storm. Kristine O'Connell George uses words such as "workbench," "cranks," "hitches," and "engines" in her poem "Monkey Wrench." You can get your students to do the same thing. Ask them to create a word storm by brainstorming any words that are connected with their object. Simply spill the words and phrases out onto paper. For example, a poem about a chair may include *velvet fabric*, *high back*, *wooden legs*, *plush seat*, *sturdy*, *strong*, *wobbly*, *living room*, or *Grandfather's favorite*. Sometimes a phrase will come to mind that is alliterative or built around a simile. In this example, students might come up with "soft, simple seat," or "as sturdy as a house of bricks." Encourage students to stretch their thinking by including appeal to the senses such as "smells-like-grandma chair." Often, students will find it easier to do a word storm around a sketch of the object.

"Monkey Wrench" uses the strength of verbs to build lines of poetry. Many lines begin with verbs such as "cranks," "bites," "juts," "tackling," and "hangs." Students can learn from this poem how an effective piece of writing is often built on powerful verbs and precise nouns. Too often students try to improve a piece of writing by adding strings of adjectives rather than examining nouns and verbs for their specificity.

The adjectives that are used are important and interesting. "Strong-jawed" used to describe "grin" is specific to a monkey wrench and the work it does. The hyphenated adjective is unique and can stand alone to describe the noun. No other adjective is needed. It is important to point out to students that the author never uses more than one or two adjectives to describe a noun.

Older students may want to investigate the two lines that use paired adjectives with no commas to separate them ("stubborn rusted bolts" and "wide silver chin"). These adjectives are called cumulative adjectives, indicating that they cannot be interchanged or that the conjunction "and" could not be added and make good sense. Students can look for additional examples of cumulative adjectives and compare them with coordinate adjective pairs (adjectives that can change places with no change to the meaning of the sentence, such as *ripe red* apple).

"Monkey Wrench" uses an interesting line break, placing the word "yawning" all by itself even though it could easily fit on the line above. Ask students why they think the poet did this and if they think it improved the poem. One reason for this placement might be to emphasize how hard the monkey wrench worked and how tired he is by drawing attention to the one-word line. Your students may come up with other reasons. The idea is just to get them thinking and making hypotheses about the work writers do.

❖   ❖   ❖   ❖   ❖

## The Winter Tree
*by Douglas Florian*

The winter tree
Is fast asleep.
She dreams, in reams
Of snow knee-deep,
Of children climbing
Up her trunk,
Of white-tailed deer
And gray chipmunk,
Of picnics,
Hammocks,
And short sleeves,
  And leaves
    And leaves
      And leaves
        And leaves.

**Figure 5.1** Chart for long "e" sound patterns

## Reading Connections

Students can enjoy this poem for the rhythm and rhyme. They can find examples of internal rhyme such as "She dreams, in reams" and end rhyme pairs such as "trunk" and "chipmunk" and "sleeves" and "leaves." This structure makes it a fun poem for young students to hear and recite. The repetition of the word "leaves" is enjoyable for students to say out loud.

"The Winter Tree" uses many words with the long "e" vowel sound. Here is a chance to review the different ways to represent the sound of long "e" in spelling. One way to do this is to chart and categorize the different words that contain a long "e" sound. See Figure 5.1 for an example from a group of Rose's second graders.

Notice that the chart contains some words not found in the poem. After charting the words from the poem, Rose encouraged the students to think of other words that contained the same spelling pattern. They then examined the placement of the spelling pattern—sometimes it came at the end of the word, sometimes in the middle. The students continued to add words they found in their independent reading and discussed how their discoveries about these vowel patterns helped them to decode. One student noticed that "sleeves," "leaves," and "please" had an extra "e" at the end. These two words then became a new category with "breeze" and "sneeze" added. Words from the chart were then used for independent sorting. Older students could extend this investigation by considering the change in spelling from the singular "leaf" to the plural "leaves."

Students can wear their detective hats while reading this poem and find the clues to help them make several inferences. For example, if the tree is dreaming about picnics, hammocks, and short sleeves, she is probably dreaming about summertime. The last lines show us that the poem is told in the voice of a deciduous tree, not a pine tree. We might also conclude that the setting of this poem is well into the winter season since the snow is knee-deep and the tree is beginning to long for summer.

As readers we know the poem is written in the third person but the poet uses the pronouns "she" and "her" instead of "it" and "its," making the tree come alive for the reader. The persona poem allows readers to make personal connections, especially if they live in an area of harsh and snowy winters. They too dream of warmer weather.

## Writing Connections

In "The Winter Tree," Douglas Florian effectively creates several snapshots of setting using a list. Students can once again see the power of nouns in forming pictures and helping the reader to visualize. For example, the poet does not just say "animals," he gives us a clearer picture by talking about "white-tailed deer" and a "gray chipmunk." Anyone who has ever rested in a hammock will not need any other words to describe it in order to conjure up the picture. If your students aren't familiar with this word, find a copy of *Old Elm Speaks: Tree Poems* by Kristine O'Connell George and share the poem "Between Two Trees" with them. This poem is accompanied by a great illustration of a hammock.

Students will notice the use of hyphenated adjectives in this poem. Usually adjectives appear right in front of the noun they describe. In the lines

> She dreams, in reams
> Of snow knee-deep,

the poet places the adjective after the noun it describes. You might ask your student writers why the poet did not say "knee-deep snow" instead. Some students may offer an explanation of rhyme. Others may talk about the way this adjective placement emphasizes how much snow is on the ground and varies the structure of a sentence—almost adding to its poetic posture.

Sometimes when poets write they vary the form of a word to better fit the rhyme, rhythm, or to simply play with language. In other words, they take "poetic license." Florian takes this liberty in the line "And gray chipmunk." We want to say "chipmunks" but that wouldn't fit the rhyme with "trunk." Another great example of how poets invent language when they need it can be found in "Tree Traffic" in *Old Elm Speaks: Tree Poems* by Kristine O'Connell George ("treeway" and "squirreled").

Poetry uses effective repetition to make a statement, to help the reader remember a big idea, or to create a certain rhythm. Words, phrases, and lines can be repeated. In "The Winter Tree" the repetition of the phrase "and leaves" helps the reader visualize a summer tree with a profusion of green leaves. Invite your students to return to their notebooks and look for places in prose or poetry they have already written and ask them to find places where repetition is effective. We want them to understand the difference between purposeful repetition and redundancy. There are many examples of effective repetition of words and phrases in *I Didn't Do It* by Patricia MacLachlan and Emily MacLachlan Charest. The poems, all written in the voice of dogs, are fun to read and easy to imitate.

❖   ❖   ❖   ❖   ❖

### Letter to the Sun
*by Joyce Sidman*

Dear Sun:
It's so wet.

The meadow has turned to bog.
Chill, sinking, squishy sog.

We long for your face, Sun.
We crave your rays,
those
   long,
      lovely,
         honey-colored days.

O Dear Sun,
we're huddled in our buds,
waiting to bloom.

Please come soon . . .
the only ones still singing
are the frogs.

*Signed,*_____

## Reading Connections

Sidman's poem is like a riddle for students, written in a friendly-letter format without a signature. Students can make inferences by using the poet's description of setting. As the poem progresses, the poet's clues become more focused: "we're huddled in our buds, waiting to bloom" so that the readers' inferences lead to the final conclusion that the flowers are writing the letter.

If it is appropriate, ask students to make connections with a science unit on plants. Perhaps your students will remember learning about photosynthesis or a time when they had a chance to grow a tomato plant or a flower from seeds. Their connection to their background knowledge will deepen their understanding of this poem and why the flowers need the sun as well as the rain.

Students can find the rhymes and create word families using the end chunk. It is important that students use this skill when they are trying to decode a word. For example, if they can read "log," "frog," and "hog," then they should be able to sound out "bog" and "sog"— even though they are unfamiliar with these words (the poet has created the word "sog" from the word *soggy* to maintain the rhyme).

Ask your students to draw a picture of the setting and characters who are writing this letter. Give them time to color and label their drawings. Then post them and compare the pictures. How are they alike? Different? Ask the artists in your classroom to explain what words in the poem helped them to form this picture in their mind's eye.

It is sometimes difficult for students to grasp the concepts of tone and mood. Tone is set by the author's attitude toward the topic, while mood is the overall feeling that the reader gets from the text. Sidman sets the tone through her description of setting and word choice. She talks about the "chill" and refers to the meadow as a "bog." The flowers address the sun in a formal, polite manner ("O Dear Sun"). They make their request in a respectful voice using the word "please." The tone of this piece is serious and formal. As readers we use the devices we find in the text, in this case, description of setting ("sinking, squishy bog"), the monologue of the flowers ("the only ones still singing are the frogs"), and images created by phrases such as "huddled in our buds" to establish a rather gloomy mood that fits most readers' notions of prolonged rainy days.

Personification is a literary device often used in poetry as well as other genres. If students cannot identify its use, they will miss the subtle implications of story and poetry. Here in "Letter to the Sun," Sidman creates lines that use human emotions and attributes them to the flowers waiting to bloom. She has them longing and craving the sun's face and its warm rays. In addition, the flowers address the sun as if the sun were a person, using the greeting "Dear Sun" and "O Dear Sun" the way you would write a greeting ending in someone's name. Just the idea that flowers can write a letter to the sun is personification.

## Writing Connections

"Letter to the Sun" begs for a discussion of the friendly-letter format, including the use of appropriate punctuation and spacing. The greeting of the letter is written like a salutation ending in a colon. This punctuation mark is used in a business format; however, Sidman's poem sounds more like a formal friendly letter though the flowers are making a request. Students can identify the greeting, body, and closing. The signature is a blank line so the students can guess who authored the letter. (See the Your Turn Lesson: Writing a Persona Poem in the Form of a Letter at the end of this chapter.)

What an interesting poem to study Sidman's line breaks! She takes the idea of "long, lovely, honey-colored days" and extends it over three lines so that it, too, becomes long, important, and thought-provoking. "It's so wet" stands alone after the greeting—a simple statement that captures the big idea the flowers are trying to relay to Sun.

Other conventions to study include contractions ("it's," "we're") and the use of a comma of address ("We long for your face, Sun."). A well-placed ellipsis in the final verse helps the reader pause and linger on the request made by the flowers ("Please come soon . . .").

Sidman included some rhyme ("rays" and "days") and near rhyme ("bloom" and "soon") and took poetic license to create a rhyme by inventing "sog" to rhyme with "bog." Assonance can be found in the repeated vowel sounds in "chill, sinking, squishy sog" and "huddled in our buds." It is interesting to note that Sidman does not end her final verse with a rhyme, perhaps because the poem ends with a serious observation.

It's always important to discuss word choice in a poem since most poems that students will write will be fairly short. Making every word count often means that students roll up their sleeves and put some hard work into the revision process. First, they can take a look at their verbs and nouns for specificity. Sidman uses strong verbs like "crave" and "huddled" as well as specific nouns like "meadow" and "bog." A sprinkling of well-placed adjectives include the hyphenated adjective "honey-colored," demonstrating to students just how effective a hyphenated adjective can be. The flowers are talking and referring to honey. It makes the reader think of bees collecting honey from flowers on bright, sunny days. It is a unique way to refer to days filled with sunshine. Sidman's well-chosen adjectives also create alliteration ("long, lovely" and "sinking, squishy sog").

## Your Turn Lesson

# WRITING A PERSONA POEM IN THE FORM OF A LETTER

It is always important for students to think of audience when doing any kind of writing, but especially when learning about letter writing. Writing a persona poem in the form of a letter can help students think about audience and provide a more authentic experience to review and practice the elements of letter writing.

**Hook:** Return to the poem "Letter to the Sun" in *Butterfly Eyes and Other Secrets of the Meadow* by Joyce Sidman. Invite students to examine what the poet includes in the body of her letter poem—a description of what is happening, information about the sun and how much the flowers need her, and an invitation to do something.

**Purpose:** *Writers, just like Joyce Sidman wrote a letter to the sun in the voice of the flowers, today I will show you how you can write a persona poem in the form of a letter. You will pretend to be an object or living thing and write a letter poem to someone or something in its voice.*

**Brainstorm:** Ask students to brainstorm things they might like to pretend to be such as everyday objects, something in nature, an animal, or things tied to a curriculum area. Examples might include a pencil, hook, apple tree, squirrel, dog, butterfly, rose, bee, triangle, cylinder, magnet, prism, or cumulus cloud. As students offer suggestions you can also have them think about who or what that thing might want to write a letter to.

**Model:** First, choose something from the list, then think aloud about who or what you would want to write to and why. Here is an example Rose used with a group of students.

*I've been having a terrible time with the squirrels in my back yard lately. They want to get the seeds in the birdfeeder, so they hang on the perch until it falls off. Then the birds can't get to the seeds. Most of the time the birds and squirrels don't seem to mind each other, but I'm thinking the birds might want to write to the squirrels asking them to be more careful.*

Then she wrote this poem in front of the students.

Dear Squirrels:
It's winter.

We know it's hard for all of us
    to find food.

We don't mind sharing the birdseed.
You are good company for us
    in the cherry tree.

But Squirrels,
When you hang on our perch and knock it
    off . . .
        the . . .
            feeder . . .
We have nowhere to stand.

Please be careful . . .
Leave the feeder intact.
(We'd appreciate a few more seeds, too!)

Your friends,
The Birds

**Shared/Guided Writing:** Choose another subject from the list and follow the same procedure with the class. Here's an example from a shared experience:

Dear Spring:
It's February.

I am feeling a little cold.
Winter has been cruel.

My toes are freezing under all the snow.
I dream . . .
    of your warm breezes
        bringing new life to my branches.

I dream  . . . of Robin returning to build her nest
   safely hidden
      among my delicate white flowers.

O Spring,
Please hurry.

Love,
The Apple Tree

If students need additional support they can work in pairs or triads to create additional persona letter poems.

**Independent Writing:** Students can return to the brainstormed list for ideas in writing their own persona poem letters. They can continue to brainstorm ideas for the topics listed, or add new topics and ideas to their writer's notebooks.

**Reflection:** Ask students to reflect on how the activity worked for them.

*How did writing a persona poem letter help you think about audience and form?*
*Was it easy or hard to write in the voice of something else? What strategies did you use to help you write in another voice?*
*What was the tone of your letter? What did you do to create that tone?*
*Were you trying to persuade someone to think a certain way or make something happen? How did your choice of words help define your purpose clearly?*

**Option:** If students have difficulty writing in the voice of another object, animal, or person, have them write in their own voice first. They can write a poem of address where they speak directly to the squirrels or tree or ocean, and so on, but in their own voice. Transitioning to persona writing might then be easier for them.

# Your Turn Lesson

## WRITING A PERSONA POEM AS AN APOLOGY

One way to introduce students to persona poetry is through an apology poem. It can be fun, lighthearted, and relate to areas of the curriculum.

**Hook:** Read William Carlos Williams' famous poem "This Is Just to Say." You might want to establish some background knowledge of this poet and generate more interest in writing apology poems by reading *River of Words: The Story of William Carlos Williams* by Jen Bryant, a picture book biography. See the end pages in this book for "This Is Just to Say" and other poems by Williams. You may want to have a discussion about the absence of punctuation in this poem and why the poet wrote it in this way. Ask the students to imagine his target audience. Is this poem for a family member, perhaps his wife? Options include poems found in *Forgive Me, I Meant to Do It: False Apology Poems* by Gail Carson Levine or *This Is Just to Say: Poems of Apology and Forgiveness* by Joyce Sidman.

**Purpose:** *Writers, today we are going to have some fun writing an apology poem and imitating the structure of William Carlos Williams. You will assume a new persona by "walking around in the skin" of something else.*

**Brainstorm:** Ask students to brainstorm a list of objects, animals, or book characters as a two-column chart. As students offer suggestions you can also have them think about whose voice they want to write in and who or what their target audience might be (who or what they might want to write a letter to). For example, your chart could look something like this:

| Voice | Target Audience |
|---|---|
| mosquito | little boy |
| puppy | owner |
| bee | flower |
| sneaker | foot |
| pencil | writer |
| wolf | Red Riding Hood |
| Grinch | the Whos |
| magnet | nail |
| farmer | bats |

**Model:** Choose something from the list and create a model based on William Carlos Williams' poem. Students will notice that the poem begins with an explanation and ends with an apology and description appealing to the senses. As you model, borrow some lines such as "This is just to say" and begin each verse with a borrowed stem such as "I have," "and which," and "Forgive me." Those stems will provide a scaffold for students to initially follow. Here's an example from a farmer to the bats:

## This Is Just to Say

I have sprayed
the beetles and grasshoppers
that were in
my cornfield

and which
you were probably
going to gobble up
for dinner

Forgive me
they were a nuisance
so numerous
and so destructive

**Shared/Guided Writing:** Students can work with a partner or a small group to write their apology poem. Students should begin by determining the voice the poem will be written in, the target audience, and, finally, the subject matter. Once they have completed their poem, they could write a response in the voice of the target audience (dialogue poems). If you are going to try this out you might want to read some examples from Joyce Sidman's *This Is Just to Say: Poems of Apology and Forgiveness* to the entire class. (See the examples from fourth graders and their teacher, Karen Drew, in this chapter).

**Independent Writing:** Students can try writing their own apology poems. They can pick from the brainstormed list or examine any expert lists they might have in their writer's notebook. For example, a hockey player may write in the voice of a hockey stick talking to the puck. Students may first try out this format writing in their own voice to a family member or friend.

**Reflection:** Ask students to reflect on how the activity worked for them.

*Does your poem use humor or another emotion to appeal to your reader?*

*Would your poem be received as a sincere apology? Why or why not?*

*Can you think of other synonyms for the adjectives in the last verse of your poem?*

*What words did you choose to include that helped your reader identify the voice this poem was written in?*

# CHAPTER 6

# Poetry for Two Voices

### the drip
#### by Will Mowery

| | |
|---|---|
| drip . . . | |
| Drip . . . | ooommph! |
| drip drip . . . | ooooommmph! |
| drip . . . | oh this dratted . . . |
| drip . . . | oomph! can't get this faucet . . . |
| drip drip drip . . . | to stop . . . |
| | drip . . . |
| | . . .ping |
| Drip . . . | Oh, go drip yourself! |
| Drip . . . | DRIP! DRIP! DRIP! |
| Drip . . . | |
| . . . drip . . . drip . . . drip . . .* | DRIP! DRIP! DRIP! DRIP! DRIP! DRIP! DRIP! |
| . . . . . . | hey, wait . . . |
| . . . | I think maybe . . . |
| . . . | Yes! It . . . |
| Drip . . . | didn't stop. |
| Drip . . . | ooommph! |
| drip drip drip . . . | ooooooommmmph! |
| CrrraaAAACK! | EEEOWWWWWW!! |

* Voice 1 says one drip with second, fourth, and sixth drip of voice 2.

Poems for two voices create unique opportunities to blend reading, writing, speaking, and listening into one activity. Mentor texts such as *Joyful Noise: Poems for Two Voices* by Paul Fleischman or *Messing Around on the Monkey Bars* by Betsy Franco house poems that serve as wonderful examples for students to read, perform, and imitate in their own writing. This kind of poetry can also be used to practice skills involving higher-order thinking such as comparison and contrast. After students read a poem that compares and contrasts two animals, people, biomes, or events, they can take the ideas presented in the poem and rewrite it in a two-voice poem. Of course, performance is the end goal in most cases since poetry is meant to be shared by reading aloud. The students make decisions about who is going to read each voice and how the lines will be read. These poetry performances can "go on the road" to other classes in the same or different grade levels.

Paul Fleischman's *Joyful Noise: Poems for Two Voices* and *I Am Phoenix: Poems for Two Voices* are good places to start for students in upper elementary and middle school. Younger students will enjoy the poems in the You Read to Me, I'll Read to You series by Mary Ann Hoberman. These books use the poem for two voices as a poetic genre, so you can immerse the students in reading and performing the poems before you ask students to write them. While this type of poem is composed to be read aloud by two readers, some can be created for three or more voices. A good example of multiple-voice poetry is *Big Talk: Poems for Four Voices* by Paul Fleischman. In the poems for two voices genre, lines of poetry are spoken by the individual reader separately, and the speakers take turns going back and forth between the voices. It is important to note that some lines are composed to be said out loud simultaneously by both speakers. In Sara Holbrook's *Weird? (Me, Too!) Let's Be Friends*, poems often have text printed in blue type and centered at the end of the poem where the two voices become one. Sometimes, poets use boldface or italic print to indicate that the lines are read simultaneously by both speakers, and sometimes the readers recognize when they read together because the lines are directly opposite each other in the two-column poem. Poetry for two voices requires some rehearsal by students before they can perform.

Perhaps the easiest way to transition from reading poems for two voices to writing poems for two voices is to take a poem and rewrite it as a poem for two voices. (See the Your Turn Lesson at the end of this chapter.) Another option is to revisit a children's book that has a seesaw structure and rewrite it using the same words as a poem for two voices. Some good choices may include *Tough Boris* by Mem Fox, *Fortunately* by Remy Charlip, *My Mom Travels a Lot* by Caroline Feller Bauer, and *That's Good! That's Bad!* by Margery Cuyler. Another literature connection is *I Am the Dog I Am the Cat* by Donald Hall. Other books that can be used as an introduction to writing persuasion and argument and can readily be written in a two-voice poem format are *Earrings!* by Judith Viorst, *Dear Mr. Blueberry* by Simon James, and *I Wanna Iguana* by Karen Kaufman Orloff.

"I Like" by Mary Ann Hoberman is a mentor poem that can be used at the beginning of the year when students are first being introduced to each other. Students can work in partners and use a Venn diagram to organize their thinking about ways they are the same and different. The Venn diagram can help them place differences on opposing lines that contrast a particular trait. For example, if one student says, "I have brown eyes," the other student may write, "I have green eyes." Students can brainstorm a list of their favorite things and favorite activities as a way to get started. Together they can decide which items on their list they will compare and contrast. Younger students can create a face for each diagram circle and write their names above the circle. The teacher can then display the faces at eye level as a way to have students learn about each other and "read" the classroom. From their Venn diagrams they can write their two-voice poems. For younger children, a scaffold may be helpful. For example, the first line for each speaker may talk about a difference, the second line about a similarity, and so on until the poem is finished. Here's an example:

| | |
|---|---|
| I have yellow hair. | |
| | I have black hair. |
| I love to run! | I love to run! |
| I have a cat. | |
| | I have a parrot. |
| I like | I like |
| chocolate-chip cookies. | chocolate-chip cookies. |
| I want to be a mom. | |
| | I want to be a fireman. |
| I like recess. | I like recess. |

In Bruce Bloome's fourth-grade classroom, students studied the two-voice poem for the first time. Bruce read *Guess Who My Favorite Person Is* by Byrd Baylor. Baylor's books are all written in a unique style, lyrical and rhythmical, with beautiful illustrations and a two-column layout for the writing. This book is about two friends playing the naming game—naming their favorite things—in a dialogue that goes back and forth between the friends. There are quotation marks and other conventions of conversation, and it is easy to follow the "she said" and "I said" descriptions.

Bruce had previously shared several Byrd Baylor books, especially *I'm in Charge of Celebrations*, so he returned to this book and read it again. The students used their stop-'n'-jot notebooks to write down their observations about Baylor's craft.

The next day Bruce reread *Guess Who My Favorite Person Is* and shared his own poem, "Pet Preference," written in two voices (see Classroom Connections for this poem later in this chapter). Lynne read one of the voices so the students could hear how the poem was constructed without a visual. Next, the students looked at the poem and the layout, talking about how the lines helped the readers know who was reading and which lines were read separately or together. Bruce pulled another book, *The Seaside Switch* by Kathleen V. Kudlinski, and read it aloud. The book offers rich descriptions of the cycling of the low and high tides at the seashore. He asked the students to turn and talk about the way the author compares and contrasts the different tides and what the boy pictured in the illustrations is viewing at the ocean's edge. Then the students brainstormed a list of opposites or almost opposites that they could possibly write about in a two-voice poem format. Their list included day and night, dawn and dusk, dreams and nightmares, black and white, soft and hard, quiet and noisy, city and country, dark and bright, clean and dirty, sweet and sour, and many others.

Bruce demonstrated how he first wrote his two-voice poem as a conversation. He placed the writing on a document imager so the students could notice the conventions of creating a dialogue that is easily understood. Bruce also returned to Baylor's book, *Guess Who My Favorite Person Is*. He wanted his students to discover that Baylor focused on creating unique descriptions of favorite things, not the explanatory words often used in a conversation outside of the quotation marks. Baylor simply used either "She said" or "I said" to start the dialogue each time the speaker changed or a slight variation such as "So I said" or "But she said," instead of fussing over myriad ways to say the word "said."

Next, students chose a partner and evaluated their lists of opposites before coming to consensus about the pair they would like to describe in a two-voice poem. After they chose their topic, the students wrote their first draft in dialogue format as a conversation. They revised for specific examples and elements of craft such as alliteration, simile, metaphor, more specific nouns, and powerful verbs. The students read their conversations to different peer partners to get feedback for revision purposes. Lynne and Bruce were available to offer help with editing, reviewing and modeling conventions of conversation and Baylor's format whenever the students needed additional help. *Joyful Noise: Poems for Two Voices* and *I Am Phoenix: Poems for Two Voices* by Paul Fleischman were also available as mentor texts for the students.

When the students took their drafts to a computer to copy, Bruce had them keyboard their conversation as a two-column poem for the two-voice format. The students had already highlighted or sometimes added in and highlighted all the text that would be read together, imitating Bruce's format in his model. These lines would be placed in each column, directly across from each other on the same line. The students imitated the way Byrd Baylor created her favorite-thing-naming-game conversation. When they were finished, the students returned to the classroom to practice their poems for a performance. Eric and Joe wrote about their favorite seasons:

| | |
|---|---|
| I like summer. | I like winter |
| You like winter? | |
| | You like summer? |
| In summer, | |
| the pool is very cold, | |
| it never gets old. | |

                                        In winter,
                                        you can go sledding
                                        down the vast hill.

The summer block party
is always sure to please.

                                        Winter is like
                                        a snowball airstrike
                                        falling down on us.

Summer is
the warmest season—
you can have more play time.

                                        Summer is kind of good,
                                        but winter is better
                                        for the most.
                                        You can build forts
                                        and be a snowball-fight host.

I guess winter is cool,
but I still think
that summer is better.
You can go swimming at the beach.

                                        You can go ice skating
                                        and play ice hockey.
                                        You can go snowboarding.

In summer,
you eat cold slushies,
icy popsicles.

                                        You can bake
                                        fresh chocolate chip cookies
                                        with hot chocolate on the side.

Summer is
the best time of year.
Amusement parks and carnivals
are open.

                                        Winter is
                                        the best time of year.
                                        You can go ice fishing
                                        in the frozen lakes.

I like summer
in my opinion.

                                        I like winter
                                        in many ways.
I like summer.                          I like winter.

Poems for two voices can be written across the curriculum about anything and can serve as a way to assess understanding. In Teresa Lombardi's third-grade classroom, Emily chose to compare the characters in Andrew Clements' book *The Report Card* (see Figure 6.1 for her plan).

Madison chose to compare two widely different subjects in her poem "Polar Bear and SUV":

Figure 6.1 Emily's plan for a two-voice poem

I chomp down on fish.

        I gobble gasoline.

    You eat odd things.

I swim in the lakes and oceans.

        I ride all over the world.

    I think I would hate to do that.

I live in arctic regions.

        I live in a garage.

    I wonder what that would be like

      to live in.

        You should see the view

        from here.

Um, I think I'm fine

with the view

of my wonderful icebergs.

      My opinion is that my view is better.

I have cold air 24/7.

        I have cold air and hot air

        around me.

I swim to catch my food.

        I drive to a gas station

        to get my food.

    I wonder what it's like to get food

      that way?

I walk on all fours!

        I drive on all fours, too!

    I guess you could call us similar.

In an e-mail conversation, poet Will Mowery discussed with us his process of creating his two-voice poem "the drip." We have included it here so that you can share a poet's thinking with your students:

I once saw a cartoon in a periodical that had a guy standing in front of an artist's easel—paint brush and pallet in hand—looking over with dismay at a dripping faucet. The caption read something like "Art or plumbing, there's never enough time." That idea has stuck with me, I think, because it reminds me of how I often feel in my own life—and I'm sure others feel much the same. We have to put off the things we really want to do to focus on things that must be done. So when I started writing "the drip" it immediately demanded all my attention, and I started "ooommph!"ing over the faucet trying to get it to stop.

I didn't plan for things to progress that way as I started. It's simply what happened when I did. I wrote the word "drip," and right away I could see that annoyance was going to be nothing but trouble. But since a dripping faucet can't normally say anything other than "drip," I had the problem of figuring out how to move both sides of the conversation along. The only way I could think of to vary the faucet's end of the conversation was to vary the tempo of the drips, which is what I did; and it seemed to work fairly well.

Hence, we have the initial "drip" with an "ooommph!" in response, which results in another "drip" and a more extended "ooooommmph!" since the initial effort didn't stop the chatter of the faucet. Rather than slow down, however, the drip speeds up, which precipitates a verbal response from the second voice and on and on until the faucet finally does say something different when too much pressure is applied.

Once I got started with this piece I knew where I wanted to try to get it to go, but I didn't resolve it to my satisfaction in one sitting. This is one of those pieces I had to put aside for awhile and then go back to and fool around with a number of times until I had something I thought worked in a satisfactory way. If I work on a piece too long, I can't see it anymore from any semblance of a neutral perspective. Time away resolves that issue. It took about a month and four different drafts for me to find what I thought would work best for a student audience. I thought the first one worked pretty well up to a point, and I ended up keeping everything from the beginning and trying different endings for the other three versions, settling on the last one I wrote. (*Personal communication.*)

# CLASSROOM CONNECTIONS:
# POETRY FOR TWO VOICES

## Honeybees
### by Paul Fleischman

| | |
|---|---|
| Being a bee | Being a bee |
| | is a joy. |
| is a pain. | |
| | I'm a queen |
| I'm a worker | |
| I'll gladly explain. | I'll gladly explain. |
| | Upon rising, I'm fed |
| | by my royal attendants, |
| I'm up at dawn, guarding | |
| the hive's narrow entrance | |
| | I'm bathed |
| Then I put in an hour | |
| making wax, | |
| without two minutes' time | |
| to sit still and relax. | |
| | The rest of my day |
| | is quite simply set forth: |
| Then I might collect nectar | |
| from the field | |
| three miles north | |
| | I lay eggs, |
| or perhaps I'm on | |
| larva detail | |
| | by the hundred. |
| feeding the grubs | |
| in their cells, | |
| wishing that I were still | |
| helpless and pale. | |
| | I'm loved and I'm lauded, |
| | I'm outranked by none. |
| Then I pack combs with | |
| Pollen—not my idea of fun. | |

When I'm done
enough laying

Then, weary, I strive

I retire

to patch up any cracks
in the hive.

for the rest of the day.

Then I build some new cells,
slaving away at
enlarging this Hell,
dreading the sight
of another sunrise,
wondering why we don't
all unionize.
Truly, a bee's is the
worst
of all lives.

Truly, a bee's is the
best
of all lives.

## Reading Connections

This poem provides a chance to explore vocabulary in many different ways. You might want to try a knowledge rating scale, as discussed in Janet Allen's (1999) *Words, Words, Words: Teaching Vocabulary in Grades 4–12*. Students have the chance to think about some of the words that will appear in the reading as a way to activate prior knowledge, get ready to notice these words, and use context clues during reading. There are many different versions. Your knowledge rating scale may look something like this:

| Words | Know Well | Have Seen or Heard | No Clue |
|---|---|---|---|
| hive | | | |
| pollen | | | |
| nectar | | | |
| attendants | | | |
| outranked | | | |
| groomed | | | |

Students check the box that best describes their knowledge about each word. When you are choosing the words, it is best to limit the number to four to six words so your students are not overwhelmed by the list and can actually try to look for these words in the poem, story, or article. Students are honest when using this scale since no grade is attached to it. The words you choose should always include at least one that everyone would know and immediately recognize and another that is familiar. Your most struggling students could lose motivation to read if they don't recognize any of these words. Now you have a choice. After students compare lists with a partner or small group, they can read the poem once for enjoyment and a second time to see if they can uncover the meaning for the words that they do not know well. An alternative would include preteaching these words and using them in sentences or sometimes showing students drawings or photographs to make the meaning clear.

There are many words in this poem worth exploring. For example, you could find multiple meanings for a word like "retire." Or you could find synonyms for words like "lauded." Older students can make real-world connections to the worker bee's comment about the need to "unionize." Another interesting thing about our language is how it grows. We often take a longer word and create a shorter version of it as we do with *lab* (*laboratory*), *cab* (*taxicab*), and *exam* (*examination*). The poet refers to honeycombs as "combs." Ask your students to find other examples and create an anchor chart.

The poem is written in a way that makes it easy for students to compare and contrast the life of the queen and worker bees. The poem is written in first person for each of the voices. You might ask, "Would this poem be as effective if it were written in the poet's voice explaining the lives of the queen bee and the worker?" Students can make connections to different real-life situations—who would be the worker bees? Who would be the queen bee?

In addition to the compare and contrast structure, this poem also describes a sequence of events—the activities of the worker and the queen bees throughout the day. Students can find words that indicate time or transitions such as "upon rising," "then," "the rest of my day," "retire."

## Writing Connections

A science teacher may find this poem particularly appealing to discuss the life cycle of bees and the aspects of their lives that make them social insects. Students could try writing a similar poem using Fleischman's scaffold for other animals such as ants, wolves, lions, or termites.

As students write a poem for two voices, they need to have a clear understanding of organization—who will speak which lines, what lines will be said together, who will speak first, and whether lines will be read in different tones. Encourage students to examine the poem for places where Fleischman had his subjects speak together to say the same words or different words. There are many places where the queen bee's thoughts are interrupted by the thoughts of the worker bee. Students can try to imitate this structure in their poems as well.

Examining the word choices in this poem is perhaps one of the most valuable lessons for your young writers. You can first of all consider the number of words that are being spoken by each subject. The worker bee has more to say than the queen bee, indicating that he has much more to do. Your students will need to consider whether there is a reason for one voice to speak many more words than the other voice. The words chosen are also important for their emotional appeal. The queen bee uses words like "loved," "lauded," and "best" while the worker bee chimes in with "wishing," "dreading," "slaving." Strong verbs help emphasize the many jobs of the worker bee: "feeding," "guarding," "enlarging," "collect," "pack," "patch." The use of the adverb "truly" emphasizes the point both voices are making at the end of the poem. You and your students might make a list of other adverbs that could be used to emphasize a final point such as *surprisingly, amazingly, happily, sadly.*

❖ ❖ ❖ ❖ ❖

## Last Licks
### by Sara Holbrook

Vanilla, strawberry,
Choc-o-late,
Dripping down fingers.

           **Eat it quick.**

Two scoops
in the sunshine

           **means race to the finish.**

Pause for one moment,

           **the treat will diminish**

into rivers down arms,

           **streams between fingers,**

puddles on toes,
ice cream never lingers.

           **What sticks on the nose**
           **or drips down the chin**

are sweet taste sensations

           **that don't make it in**
to the mouth.           **to the mouth.**
Lick.           **Lick.**
Lick.           **Lick.**

          **QUICK!**
        **This cone's going south.**

## Reading Connections

A great way to introduce this poem is to ask your students to predict what a poem titled "Last Licks" could be about. You could choose to write four or five words from the poem on the board such as "scoops," "sunshine," "eat," "chin," and "lick." Ask the students to use these words to create a nutshell prediction for this poem. Be sure to have them imagine what is happening in the poem. They can even create a drawing and label it or write a caption. Then share the poem and ask them to decide if their prediction was accurate and why.

"Last Licks" can be used with younger students to teach or reinforce rhyming words. Have them listen for pairs like "fingers-lingers," "finish-diminish," and "nose-toes" as well as others. Students can think of additional words to go with each pair.

The poem concludes with the line "This cone's going south." Students can use inference to help them draw a conclusion about the meaning of this term and what is happening in this poem. They can research the origin of "going south" and how it is used in different connotations. Make connections to idioms the students are familiar with and explore the meaning of some unfamiliar ones. Some good resources to use are *My Momma Likes to Say* and *My Teacher Likes to Say* by Denise Brennan-Nelson, and *There's a Frog in My Throat* by Loreen Leedy.

Your student readers can discuss what advice the poet is giving and how the poet feels about eating ice cream. How does she establish a sense of urgency? Students should notice the word "quick" written in all caps followed by an exclamation point and words like "race," "quick," and the repetition of the word "lick."

## Writing Connections

Just like using all capitals to help the reader know that a word or certain words should be spoken in a loud voice, a writer can use other signals such as hyphens between the syllables of a word to emphasize it or let the reader know it should be said more slowly as Holbrook does with "choc-o-late."

There are many things to notice and imitate such as the poet's use of alliteration in "scoops in the sunshine" and "drips down," and strong verbs such as "lick," "streams," "puddles," "sticks," and "drips." Ask your students to look at the use of "puddles" and "streams" as verbs rather than nouns. This unexpected use makes the poem more interesting.

The show-not-tell rich description helps readers form pictures in their mind throughout the reading of this poem. Students may imitate writing a poem for two voices that describes a different process such as getting everybody ready before yelling, "Surprise!" at a party or watching a sunrise or sunset.

As students write, they need to be aware of the length and types of sentences they are creating. Short sentences add to the sense of urgency in this poem. Holbrook uses commands throughout the poem—sometimes just one word on a line.

❖   ❖   ❖   ❖   ❖

## Sparrows
### by Paul Fleischman

| | |
|---|---|
| Sparrows everywhere | Sparrows everywhere |
| There's sparrows | There's sparrows |
| everywhere | everywhere |
| They're | They're |
| squabbling | flitting |
| flitting | singing |
| singing | squabbling |
| Sharp-tailed | |
| | found in marshes |
| Henslow's | |
| | note white eye-ring |
| Lincoln's | |
| | fond of thickets |
| Vesper | |
| | white tail feathers |
| | visible while perching. |
| Sparows everywhere | Sparrows everywhere |
| They're | They're |
| flying | flirting |
| chirping | flying |
| flirting | chirping |
| | Seaside |
| feeds on insects | |
| | Cassin's |
| sings in flight | |
| | Clay-colored |
| bird of brushland | |
| | Ipswich |
| found at dunes from | |
| Cape Cod south to Georgia. | |

Sparrows
every-
where there's
squabbling
flitting
singing
sparrows
every-
where there's
sparrows
everywhere.

Sparrows
every-
where there's
squabbling
sparrows
flirting
flying
chirping
sparrows
everywhere.

## Reading Connections

As a reader you must first decide how this poem will be read. Before you choose a partner for a second voice, you would probably scan both columns simultaneously and notice where the words are the same, different, or repeated in each column. This is definitely a poem that needs more than one read to understand it and lots of reads before performing it. Your students will notice that many sections of this poem require the two voices to read together even if the words are different. You might ask your students why the poet chose to do this. The point Fleischman is making is stated at the beginning and the end of this poem—sparrows are everywhere. The voices speaking at the same time help us hear many sparrows and understand the message.

Attention to setting in this poem also reinforces the message. The poet speaks of biomes such as marshes, brushland, dunes, and thickets. Here's a chance to fill in the holes in background knowledge. Depending on where students live or what they have studied, knowledge of biomes or ecosystems could vary greatly. It is important to remember that in order to use reading strategies effectively, a student must have the schema, or background knowledge, to serve as a link to understanding.

The nomenclature is all about birds including the sounds they make—"squabbling," "singing," "chirping"—and their actions—"flitting," "flirting," "perching," "flying." Word study can include examining the shades of meaning of these words. What is the difference between "squabbling" and "singing"? What are the birds doing when they are "flitting" or "flying"? What does the poet mean when he describes them as "flirting"? Students can draw pictures to help them visualize what is going on and help them better understand the shades of meaning.

## Writing Connections

Immediately students will notice the use of proper nouns in this poem. Although students seem to steer away from them, proper nouns lend a sense of authenticity to any piece of writing. It makes the author seem more credible. It is particularly important to use proper nouns when writing an informational piece or poem. Students may have to do some research before writing a poem such as this one.

The content of this poem is built on a rich description of what sparrows look like, where they are found, and what they are doing. Telling details are simple but help the reader distinguish one kind of sparrow from the other. Hyphenated words—"clay-colored," "sharp-tailed"—are specific and are a more unique way for a writer to use adjectives.

The poem as a whole is alliterative, including many words that begin with the sound of "s" or "f"—two soft sounds. Is there a reason for this choice?

The poem is framed with the line "sparrows everywhere," which is repeated several times throughout the poem. Students can choose a line for effective repetition that they feel needs to be echoed throughout the poem. Songwriters do this all the time, and writers of stories as well. The most important thing is to know why you are doing so and that it is purposeful, not redundant.

❖　❖　❖　❖　❖

### Backboard Rap
*by Betsy Franco*

| | |
|---|---|
| bounce, bounce | |
| bounce, bounce | Dribble, dribble, |
| bounce, bounce | Pass to Trish. |
| bounce, bounce | Shoot a basket. |
| bounce, bounce | Hear the swish! |
| bounce, bounce | Dribble, dribble, |
| bounce, bounce | Pass to Vin. |
| bounce, bounce | Hit the backboard. |
| bounce, bounce | Up and in! |
| bounce, bounce | Dribble, dribble, |
| bounce, bounce | Take a shot! |
| bounce, bounce | There's the buzzer. |
| bounce, bounce | **Yeah! We're hot!** |
| bounce, bounce | |
| bounce, bounce | |
| bounce | |

## Reading Connections

This poem makes a great mentor text for this genre because it can be read in so many ways and as a two-voice or multiple-voice poem. The fact that it is called a "rap" brings rhythm to the forefront. We can hear the sound of the basketball as it bounces across the court and hits the backboard, and we can visualize the plays as we read. This poem adds a layer to fluency because it is energetic and fast. The sentences are short and great for students to practice meaningful chunking. There should be no pause in the three-word sentences. Students need to be able to read the punctuation correctly in this poem. There are quite a few exclamatory sentences including an interjection. A comma between the words "bounce, bounce" helps students match their rhythm to the second speaker. Franco uses variation in print to define her different voices. Furthermore, the first voice fades at the end of the poem as indicated by the smaller print.

In our opinion, this poem is best read if one or several voices continue to keep the rhythm going with the words "bounce, bounce" while someone else is speaking the other lines. For performance purposes, one or two students could actually bounce a basketball while the poem is being performed. Or, you could record the sound of the basketball being bounced in a continual rhythm and play it while the poem is being performed. Additionally, you could videotape students playing a basketball game with muted sound to provide a background for the performing poets.

Students can have fun with this poem while doing some skill work such as an investigation into short "i" words in one- and two-syllable words. Students can also practice skills for breaking apart two-syllable words that are compound words ("backboard") and words that have two consonants nestled between vowels ("basket," "buzzer").

You can point out the importance of nomenclature in this poem about basketball. The vocabulary in this poem relates to the game: "dribble," "pass," "shoot," "backboard," "buzzer." Students can use their background knowledge to understand the meaning of the words in this particular context. For example, "dribble" has a different meaning in basketball than it does in the context of food or drink. Students can think of other ways to use some of these words. A "buzzer" in school signals that classes are about to change or that it is dismissal time. A "pass" is needed to leave the classroom. Students can start to understand how important it is to use the entirety of a piece in order to apply context clues. Vocabulary work using context clues can be extended by asking students to bring in sports articles from a newspaper or magazine and choosing several key words that they can explain to a partner or the class using the entirety of the piece to get at the meanings. Again, we can have discussions to fill in the necessary background knowledge a reader must have to fully comprehend the articles in the sports section of a newspaper or magazine. Poems can serve as the stimulus for myriad discussions that build background knowledge for our students.

The last three lines of the second speaker call on the reader to make an inference and then draw a conclusion. The students will infer that the buzzer is signaling the end of the game. The interjection "Yeah!" probably means that the team made the final shot to score and win the game. This thinking is reinforced by the slang term, "We're hot!" and by the first speaker's voice fading. It might be interesting to explore the origin of the slang term and other similar idioms such as "in hot water," "in the hot seat," "hot off the press," "hot and bothered," "hot on the trail," "in hot pursuit," and "blow hot and cold." Word work like this is particularly useful for English language learners who often have difficulty making meaning when unfamiliar idioms are used or words are used in an unfamiliar context.

## Writing Connections

You might return to the work you did in reading workshop with word collecting to write poems around the nomenclature of another sport, hobby, or future career. Students can create lists of words or phrases around a particular activity they enjoy viewing and/or doing. Encourage students to add to their list before they start to imagine their poem by collecting newspaper articles, magazine articles, and books about their subject matter. They can decide what might be a repeating phrase read by one speaker to keep the rhythm going. For example, a poem about horseback riding may repeat the words "trot, trot" while the second speaker describes the action. Or, a poem about swimming could repeat the words "stroke, stroke."

In a second grade classroom Rose had the students brainstorm activities they enjoy doing. They shared and chose jumping rope because it was something they were all doing in gym class. First, the students drew pictures of the activity and labeled or wrote captions for their drawings. Then, collectively, they created a word storm around the phrase "jumping rope" using the words from their captions and labels. Their list included *smack, slap, jump, hop, miss, turn the rope, take a turn, double dutch, high or low, with a partner, jump right in,* and *swish-swish*. Rose talked to the young writers about the importance of effective repetition to keep the beat in "Backboard Rap" and suggested they try to do the same thing in their shared poem. They chose "smack, smack" as the repeated phrase for the first speaker to help keep the rhythm of the poem. Rose helped them return to the mentor text to notice how the poet used short sentences beginning with a verb. Together they came up with the following poem for two voices:

### Jump Rope Rap

| | |
|---|---|
| smack, smack | |
| smack, smack | Turn the rope. |
| smack, smack | Jump right in. |
| smack, smack | High and low. |
| smack, smack | Out you go! |
| smack, smack | |

Rose divided the class into two groups, and they had lots of fun performing the poem. Afterward, they reflected on how the short sentences kept the pace fast and helped them keep the rhythm. The unexpected rhyme added to the enjoyment of reading this poem aloud. Although Rose did not ask for rhyme, it was interesting that her students figured out a way to include it.

"Blackboard Rap" is a small-moment story told through a poem for two voices. This kind of poem may become a vehicle for relating a story or retelling a familiar story like "The Three Little Pigs" or *The Very Hungry Caterpillar* by Eric Carle. The You Read to Me, I'll Read to You books by Mary Ann Hoberman are good mentor texts for this extension activity.

For older students you can explore a grammar connection by talking about the different kinds of sentences in this poem—declarative, imperative, and exclamatory. Explore the relationship between subject and predicate in the imperative sentences that start with a verb and have a subject (you) that is understood.

❖　❖　❖　❖　❖

## Pet Preference
### by Bruce Bloome

I love animals!
Cats!
Did you say dogs?

Yuck!
Cats are wonderful pets!

Cats are loving, gentle friends
who sit on your lap
and purr with affection.
Can your dog do that?

I love animals!
Dogs!

Did you say cats?
Yuck!

They're not as good as dogs!
What good is a cat?

Who wants a cat on their lap?
They shed fur
all over your clothes,
and they have claws.
Dogs will curl up
by your feet,
greet you at the door with a
wonderfully wagging tail.
Cats are too independent!

Too independent?!
I think you mean
*intelligent*!
Cats are royal,
one-time friends to royalty.

          Dogs are loyal, protectors of
          presidents and princesses.

Cats are graceful, gifted gliders,
moving graciously from room to room.

          Dogs are powerful plodders,
          pulling sleds through piles of snow.

Cats are stealthy, securing your home
from mice and rats, silent sentries
always on guard.

          Dogs are champions,
          parading like models
          moving down the runway.

Cats are prideful,
preening their fur
until it is
soft as goose down.

          I love dogs, and I guess
          cats are okay.

Yeah, dogs aren't bad,
but cats are the best!
I love animals!          I love animals!

## Reading Connections

Bruce's poem can help students understand point of view and concepts of perspective and perception. The poem takes two common house pets and creates a conversation between two voices that expound the virtues of the cat and the dog. The conversation is written in a way that makes it sound authentic—like children speaking. The voices make their persuasive arguments and it is interesting to note that by the end of the poem each speaker has not changed his mind but has at least considered the other person's way of thinking. They have also found something in common with *each other*—they are both animal lovers.

The poem is rich in wonderful vocabulary words to examine in a vocabulary log or through graphic organizers such as word webs and concept maps. Many words are verbs like "parading," "preening," "shed," and "securing." Other words include exact nouns like "plodders," "champions," "protectors," and "sentries."

Research activities could include finding the historical connotations around some of the images created in the poem. For example, "Dogs are powerful plodders, pulling sleds through piles of snow" conjures up images of the Iditarod and text-to-text connections with Gary Paulsen's *Dog Song* and John Gardiner's *Stone Fox*. The line "Cats are royal, one-time friends to royalty" may be linked with studies of ancient Egypt.

The poem offers some good examples of both similes and metaphors. Other literary devices include the use of alliteration and unexpected rhyme ("royal" and "loyal").

## Writing Connections

Description is a great way to build content in any mode of writing. Bruce's descriptions of cats and dogs contain many telling details, including describing the fur on your clothes after a cat has sat on your lap, or how soft a cat feels to the touch after it has finished grooming. The adjectives are well chosen, not randomly placed. For example, he uses "powerful" to describe "plodders"—fitting, since the adjective is describing the way dogs pull sleds through lots of snow. His adjectives are interesting as well. He talks about cats as "gifted gliders." Students can talk about why the poet chose this particular word to describe how a cat moves from room to room. What picture has the poet created inside the reader's head? As students write their own poems, they can plan, draft, and revise their poem to include rich description and adjectives that are a precise fit for the noun they are describing and for the context of the sentence as a whole.

Bruce chose to both begin and end his poem with the line "I love animals!" This effective repetition, or bookend format, is sometimes used by poets, songwriters, speechmakers, and writers of prose to emphasize a point. Students can easily imitate this structure and use it as a framework to get them started with their writing.

"Pet Preference" can be used as a mini-lesson to teach students how to write conversation. In fact, Bruce wrote this poem as a conversation first and then demonstrated to the students how he would rewrite this poem in two columns as a two-voice poem. Students can reflect on the informal tone this poem takes as if the two voices are truly speaking and arguing their points.

After Bruce performed his poem with Lynne as a model for students to imitate, one of the first things the students noticed was the pair of rhyming words—"royal" and "loyal." Bruce talked about how the rhyme was unintentional when he wrote it, but he couldn't be sure that his "inner voice" had not purposely created the rhyme. He encouraged his students to find a place for unexpected rhyme as a possibility for revision. In Brianna and Aley's poem about lazy and active people, they use a splash of rhyme to add interest and keep the reader engaged:

Being lazy is fun.
Hear the
trucks go by
on the street

Being active is fun.


Hear the footsteps
from my feet.

"Pet Preference" offers opportunities to study end punctuation, even a double punctuation. The variety of sentence type adds drama to the way this poem will be published—as a performance for two voices. In their writer's notebooks students can try out other sentences that could use both a question mark and an exclamation mark. Although this kind of end punctuation is rare, it communicates a point to the reader that the voice behind the words finds something surprising and questionable.

## Your Turn Lesson

# WRITING A POEM FOR TWO VOICES FROM A ONE-VOICE POEM

Sometimes the easiest way to get started writing a poem for two voices is to start with an existing poem. Poems that are written around different points of view or that use a compare/contrast structure are good places to start. You could also take two different poems such as "What I Hate About Winter" and "What I Love About Winter" by Douglas Florian and combine them into a poem for two voices. Some poems have a repeated line such as "In Time of Silver Rain" by Langston Hughes that can be spoken by both voices (but not necessarily). In other poems, students may decide to repeat a line or rearrange the order of lines to fit better as a poem for two voices. There are many possibilities, but essentially any poem that students are familiar with can be used. We recommend "Song of the Dolphin" by Georgia Heard in *Creatures of Earth, Sea, and Sky* and "Explorers" in Donald Graves' *Baseball, Snakes, and Summer Squash: Poems About Growing Up*. As students read and rewrite the poem for performance, they will need to make decisions about how the words, phrases, or ideas should be divided, while still maintaining, or even enhancing, the meaning of the poem.

**Hook:** Return to some poems for two voices that your students have already studied and perhaps performed. Talk with them about how the poem is set up on the page and how the author indicates which voice speaks which words.

**Purpose:** *Writers, today I am going to show you how to rewrite a poem as a poem for two voices that you can perform with a partner.*

**Brainstorm:** If your students have been studying and/or collecting poems, chances are there is a class anthology, or the students have individual anthologies of the poems presented in class. Ask students to reread their anthologies, perhaps with a partner, and choose their favorite poems (they should not choose any poems already written as two voices). If students don't have poetry anthologies, collect a variety of poetry books and allow time for students to read and choose some favorites that they think might work well as a poem for two voices. Make a list of the class favorites and be sure to include your own.

**Model:** Choose a favorite poem, and think aloud as you rewrite it as a poem for two voices in front of the students. Here is a two-voice poem Lynne and Rose wrote from Allan Wolf's "Helping Hands" (see Chapter 3):

Hands are for taking.
                              Hands are for holding.
Hands are for shaping
                              and paper plane folding.

Hands are for grasping.
                              Hands are for shaking.
              Hands are for touching
              and shadow-play making.

Hands are for dressing,
                              buttoning,
zipping.
                              Scrambling,
buttering,
              flapper-jack flipping.

Hands are for clapping,
                              juggling,
jiggling.
              Hands are for washing
              and brushing and wiggling.

Hands are for raising,
                              walking and talking.
Catching and throwing
                              and bright sunlight blocking,
              wringing and twisting
              and turning and knocking.
Clock hands are perfect
                              for ticking
and tocking.
              But upside-down acrobat hands
              are for walking.

After composing the poem, perform it with a student partner, or divide the class in two to help you perform it.

**Shared/Guided Writing:** Choose another poem and ask the class to help you rewrite it as a poem for two voices. Another option is to choose a student partner to help you rewrite a poem in front of the class. Either way, it is important to model the negotiating process in addition to the rewriting process.

**Independent Writing:** Students can work with a partner to choose a favorite poem and re-write it for two voices. Don't be concerned if two or more groups choose the same poem. Then you will have a perfect opportunity to allow the class to examine both versions and notice the similarities and differences.

Allow students lots of time to practice their poems. Be sure to set aside some perfor-mance time, and perhaps invite another class or other guests to hear the students read their poems. The student writers can talk about their poems and why they made certain decisions. As they talk about their poems, the writers of the larger community can notice and perhaps appropriate the writing behavior of their peers.

**Reflection:** After the poems have been rewritten, ask your students to reflect on what they learned.

*Was it easy or hard to decide how to divide the poem?*
*How did you and your partner decide how the words would be divided?*
*Did you do much revision? Why or why not?*
*How did rereading the poem help you as a reader?*
*How did rewriting the poem help you as a writer?*

## Your Turn Lesson

# WRITING A POEM FOR TWO VOICES IN THE CONTENT AREAS

Poems give us a different vehicle to evaluate what our readers and writers know and understand. Students can extend their thinking by writing and producing a work that can be shared in several different ways, perhaps performing it orally or publishing it on a poetry wall. Producing pieces gives students the opportunity to practice the vocabulary of a specific content area so that they can remember and own the words. Composing a two-voice poem helps students develop skills of collaboration and negotiation to reach consensus—real-life skills that they can use later. Similar to a bio poem, this type of two-voice poem can represent a synthesis of ideas or an application of learning. Like the RAFT (Role-Audience-Form-Topic) or persona poem, the poem for two voices can be written in the voice of a mathematical concept or figure.

**Hook:** *Math Talk: Mathematical Ideas in Poems for Two Voices* by Theoni Pappas is a great resource for exploring curricular concepts as a way to reinforce or demonstrate learning in the area of mathematics. The poem "Triangles" from this book demonstrates an understanding of a triangle through the use of specific vocabulary words and characteristics of this geometric figure. You can share this poem with your students as an example and a hook to get their thinking started.

## Triangles

| | |
|---|---|
| Triangles | |
| | three-sides, |
| three vertices | three angles. |
| Triangles | |
| three non-collinear | three line segments |
| points. | joined. |
| | |
| Triangles | |
| | Scalene |
| isosceles | |
| equilateral | equiangular |
| obtuse | acute |
| right. | |

| Triangles | Triangles |
|---|---|
| large | small |
| always three sided. | always flat |
| Two sides always | |
| | greater than the third. |
| Three angles always | |
| | Total 180 degrees |
| Triangles | Triangles |

**Purpose:** *Writers, today I am going to show you how you can take your learning and write about it in the form of a two-voice poem. This poem will be used as a review or teaching tool for your peers through performance of the poem.*

**Brainstorm:** There are at least two easy ways to brainstorm for this lesson. If you are in writing workshop students can brainstorm across the curriculum to find topics to write about and share. If you are asking students to write in a particular content area, you may ask them to brainstorm specific concepts and special vocabulary that relate to your unit of study. For example, Teresa Lombardi's third graders developed a list in their writer's notebook around their study of the brain. Some of their words included *hemisphericity, neurons, synapse, right-brain, left-brain, cerebellum, cerebral, electrical charges.* Other students chose to create a Venn diagram for their brainstormed ideas (see Figure 6.2).

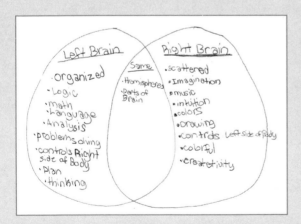

**Figure 6.2** A third grader's plan for a two-voice poem about the brain

**Model:** Choose something from your brainstormed list. In one fifth-grade classroom the students were studying ecosystems. Lynne chose *everglades* from their list to create a two-voice poem as a model. First, she listed several ideas that had been learned about the Everglades during the unit. Thinking aloud about her choices, she created the following poem:

## Everglades

| | |
|---|---|
| Florida's wetlands | Florida's wetlands |
| Blades of sawgrass | |
| | Palms and mangrove forests |
| Murky backwaters | |
| Slow-moving river | Slow-moving river |
| Shaped by water | Shaped by fire |
| Cattails and seagrass | |
| | Swampland and marshes |
| Recreation | Recreation |
| Fishing | |
| | Boating |
| Rare species | Rare species |
| | Manatees and panthers |
| Hawksbill turtles | |
| And snowy egrets | |
| | Wood storks |
| Alligators and crocodiles | Alligators and crocodiles |
| living side by side | living side by side |
| Delicate, changing | |
| | A place of wonder |
| Restore the Everglades . | Restore the Everglades . . . |
| keep it safe for the future. | keep it safe for the future. |

**Shared/Guided Writing:** Choose another idea from the brainstormed list and create a two-voice poem with your students. First, ask your students to create a graphic organizer such as a web in their writer's notebooks to generate lots of different thinking about the chosen topic. Students can share their organizers with partners or in small groups to help refine their thinking and generate details about content. Then they will be ready to come together for a shared writing experience with you.

**Independent Writing:** Once students are familiar with the format and procedure, you can offer this subgenre to informally assess your students' learning. Or, students may choose to create this type of poem in writer's workshop or as an alternative to reader's theater. Here are some samples from the third graders' writing about the brain:

## Brains Left and Right
### *by Frank and Brendan, Grade 3*

I am logical left brain

                    I am playful right brain

          And WE are part of your brain

I live in the left side

Of your head

                    I live in the right side

I wonder what it's like

To be playful

                    I wonder what it's like to be

                    Knowledgeable

I see analysis

                    I see imagination

I want to be playful

                    I want to be knowledgeable

         Similarly WE control

          What you do

I am Albert Einstein

                    I am Mozart

I touch your pencil

                    I touch your paintbrush

I worry about music class

                    I worry about PSSA's

I'm great at PSSA's

                    Well, I'm great at music class

        And WE both love school

## On Opposite Sides
### by Gabrielle and Travis, Grade 3

I am the logical
left brain.

                  I am the creative
                  right brain.

        Together WE make
          your brain.

I like to study.

                  I like play, play, playing
                  all day long.

        I wonder what it's
      like on the other side
        of the brain???

I excel in school.

                  I excel at painting.

I am a mathematical
wizard.

                  My music is as
                  fabulous as
                  Beethoven.

I am an addition sign.

                  I am a colorful
                  rainbow.

**Reflection:** Ask your students to think about what they learned from this writing experience.

*How did writing a two-voice poem help pull together what you learned?*
*How did collaboration help you create an effective poem?*
*What kinds of things did you negotiate with your partner?*
*What do you think is the most interesting or enjoyable thing about two-voice poetry?*
*What did you find difficult or challenging?*
*Where do you think you could use this kind of writing again?*

# CHAPTER 7

# A Treasure Chest of Books

We invite you into our library of poetry and companion books. You probably will find some of your favorites, but we hope you will discover new poems to share with your students as well. Our mentor poetry was chosen to span the work of your reading and writing classrooms. The poems often can be used in several grade levels depending on the strategies, skills, and content you are delving into in your classrooms.

We certainly believe that these poems can deepen our students' understandings of concepts, new and old, and provide a way for them to think about and connect with their innermost feelings and thoughts. The many dimensions of poetry will challenge students to layer their thinking about the world and their place in the world. Writing poetry by imitating the experts we have presented in this book and in our treasure chest will give students many opportunities to write for a larger audience and demonstrate new understandings. Natalie, a fifth-grade student in Frank Murphy's class, wrote a persona poem in the voice of a book. We thought it would be appropriate for her poem to help us introduce our treasure chest:

> I am full of information
> Sometimes I am easy to read,
> But sometimes
> You have to read between the lines.
> When people make me into a movie . . .
> I get mad!
> Why isn't the book enough?
> I mean, the movie doesn't have half as many details
> That I do!
> I wear a jacket
> But no shirt . . .
> I am a book.

# CHAPTER 1: GETTING STARTED

Goldstein, Bobbye S. Ed. 1992. *Inner Chimes: Poems on Poetry*. Honesdale, PA: Boyds Mills.
This anthology of poems celebrates poetry and features the work of Eleanor Farjeon, Karla Kuskin, Eve Merriam, Lilian Moore, Jack Prelutsky, Nikki Giovanni, and others. The wide range of poems should appeal to readers of varied ages.

Harley, Avis. 2000. "Editing the Chrysalis." In *Fly with Poetry: An ABC of Poetry*. Honesdale, PA: Wordsong.
This book contains an introduction, a two-page spread on additional poetic forms, an About the Author/Illustrator section, and several acrostic poems. Brief explanations of each type of poem at the bottom of each page make it a wonderful resource.

Heard, Georgia. 1992. "Will We Ever See?" In *Creatures of Earth, Sea, and Sky*. Honesdale, PA: Boyds Mills.
A collection of seventeen poems about animals; includes a question poem, poems for two voices, and a persona poem.

Merriam, Eve. 1962. "Lullaby." In *There Is No Rhyme for Silver*. New York: Atheneum.
A collection of poems by the author written in various styles about a variety of topics.

O'Neill. Mary. 1961. *Hailstones and Halibut Bones*. New York: Bantam Doubleday Dell.
Poems about colors that invoke all the senses and emotions.

Otten, Charlotte. 1997. *January Rides the Wind*. New York: William Morrow.
A collection of short poems for each month. This is a great resource for teaching personification.

Thomas, Patricia. 2007. *Nature's Paintbox: A Seasonal Gallery of Art and Verse*. Minneapolis, MN: Millbrook.
A picture book about the way Nature paints each season written with poetic language.

# CHAPTER 2: POETRY TO INSPIRE RESPONSE

Bagert, Brod. 1996. "My Writer's Notebook." In *School Supplies: A Book of Poems*, ed. Lee Bennett Hopkins. New York: Simon & Schuster.

This book is a collection of poems that describe school-related objects. Students will easily identify with the subjects and may be inspired to try their hand at describing other school objects in poetic form. "My Writer's Notebook" provides a wonderful example of metaphor.

Fletcher, Ralph. 2005. "Writer's Notebook." In *A Writing Kind of Day*. Honesdale, PA: Boyds Mills.

This collection of poems show how ordinary and varied subjects can provide seeds for a poem. In "Writer's Notebook," Fletcher describes an idea for a poem that he jots in his writer's notebook. Later in the book we see the poem that came from that idea ("Earth Head").

Fry, Nan. 1994. "Apple." In *The Earth Is Painted Green: A Garden of Poems About Our Planet*, ed. Barbara Brenner. New York: Scholastic.

Nature poems to heighten appreciation of the world around us.

Graves, Donald. 1996. "Summer Squash." In *Baseball, Snakes, and Summer Squash: Poems About Growing Up*. Honesdale, PA: Boyds Mills.

A collection of free-verse poems about a boy's adventures growing up; many of the poems, including "Summer Squash," are story poems.

Hughes, Langston. 1994. "Dream Dust." In *The Dream Keeper and Other Poems*. New York: Alfred A. Knopf.

Originally published in 1932, this classic collection of poems by Langston Hughes about the celebration and struggles of the African American experience contains seven additional poems and includes an introduction by Lee Bennett Hopkins.

McCord, David. 1996. "Every Time I Climb a Tree." In *A Jar of Tiny Stars*, ed. Bernice E. Cullinan. Honesdale, PA: Boyds Mills.

This book is a collection of poems from some of NCTE's award-winning poets.

McKissack, Patricia C. 2008. "Remembering." In *Stitchin' and Pullin': A Gee's Bend Quilt*. New York: Random House.

The poems in this book tell the story of the women from Gee's Bend. "Remembering" offers a simple scaffold that can be imitated in many contexts (see the Your Turn Lesson in this chapter).

***Companion pieces:***

Ewald, Wendy. 2002. *The Best Part of Me: Children Talk About Their Bodies in Pictures and Words*. New York: Little, Brown.

Greenfield, Eloise. 1986. "Keepsake." In *Honey, I Love and Other Poems*. New York: HarperCollins.

Herman, Charlotte. 2003. *The Memory Cupboard: A Thanksgiving Story*. New York: Albert Whitman.

Howard, Elizabeth Fitzgerald. 1991. *Aunt Flossie's Hats (and Crab Cakes Later)*. New York: Clarion.

Livingston, Myra Cohn. 1996. "A Book." In *School Supplies: A Book of Poems*, ed. Lee Bennett Hopkins. New York: Simon & Schuster.

Viorst, Judith. 1981. "Teddy Bear Poem." In *If I Were in Charge of the World and Other Worries*. New York: Simon & Schuster.

Woodruff, Elvira. 2006. *Small Beauties*. New York: Alfred A. Knopf.

Worth, Valerie. 1994. "Marbles." In *All the Small Poems and Fourteen More*. New York: Farrar, Straus and Giroux.

Mowery, Will. "That Reminds Me." Used by permission of the author.

**Companion pieces:**

Kirk, David. 2005. *The Listening Walk*. New York: Callaway.

Ryder, Joanne. 1993. *The Goodbye Walk*. New York: Dutton.

Showers, Paul. 1991. *The Listening Walk*. New York: HarperCollins.

Thurman, Judith. 1996. "New Notebook." In *School Supplies: A Book of Poems*, ed. Lee Bennett Hopkins. New York: Simon & Schuster.

This poem contains two similes and offers a visual way to think about writer's notebooks.

Varner, William. "The Squirrel." Used by permission of the author.

Zolotow, Charlotte. 1993. "Pigeons." In *Snippets: A Gathering of Poems, Pictures, and Possibilities*. New York: HarperCollins Children's.

A collection of poems from earlier, complete works by Zolotow. "Pigeons" is from *The Park Book*, Zolotow's first published book.

**Companion pieces:**

Zolotow, Charlotte. 1986. *The Park Book*. New York: HarperCollins. (This book was originally written and published in 1944.)

"Feed the Birds." 1964. From the movie *Mary Poppins*. Written by Richard M. Sherman and Robert B. Sherman.

## CHAPTER 3: LIST POEMS ARE FOR EVERYONE

Coatsworth, Elizabeth. 1966. "Swift Things Are Beautiful." In *Reflections on a Gift of Watermelon Pickle . . . and Other Modern Verse*, ed. Stephen Dunning, Edward Leuders, and Hugh Smith. New York: Lothrop, Lee & Shepard.

The 114 poems found in this book were specifically chosen to appeal to young readers. Includes a wide range of works by well-known and also little-known poets.

Dotlich, Rebecca Kai. 2009a. "Lost and Finds." In *Falling Down the Page: A Book of List Poems*, ed. Georgia Heard. New York: Roaring Brook.

A list poem that can generate notebook entries about things that are lost and found. Note the listings in this poem make no use of conjunctions, only commentary dashes and the ellipsis. This poem is built around nouns.

***Companion pieces for older students (middle school and up):***

Hesse, Karen. 1997. *Out of the Dust.* New York: Scholastic.

Tyler, Anne. 2005. *Breathing Lessons.* Ballantine.

———. 2009b. "Walking Home from School I See:" In *Falling Down the Page: A Book of List Poems,* ed. Georgia Heard. New York: Roaring Brook.

An example of a list poem that can serve as a scaffold for writers of all ages.

Edwards, Richard. 1994. "Useless Things." In *Poetry from A to Z: A Guide for Young Writers*, ed. Paul Janeczko. New York: Macmillan.

This book is an A-to-Z anthology of different poetry formats.

Florian, Douglas. 1999. "What I Hate About Winter" and "What I Love About Winter." In *Winter Eyes*. New York: Greenwillow.

Two great list poems that students can use to practice the compare/contrast structure and understand point of view.

Frank, John. 2003. "Signs." In *A Chill in the Air: Nature Poems for Fall and Winter.* New York: Simon & Schuster.

The poems in this book take the reader from the first signs of fall to the end of winter. Although they are not all in list form, all the poems are short snapshots that create a vivid scene in the mind of the reader.

***Companion pieces:***

Fleming, Denise. 2001. *Pumpkin Eye.* New York: Henry Holt.

Lotz, Karen. 1993. *Snowsong Whistling.* New York: Penguin.

Partridge, Elizabeth. 2002. *Moon Glowing.* New York: Dutton Children's.

George, Kristine O'Connell. 1997. "Zeke, an Old Farm Dog." In *The Great Frog Race and Other Poems.* New York: Clarion.

This collection of poetry centers around observations of small things and an appreciation of nature. The author includes different types of poems such as haiku, concrete, and free verse.

Heard, Georgia, ed. 2009. *Falling Down the Page: A Book of List Poems.* New York: Roaring Brook.

This book is a collection of list poems from a variety of poets, offering inspiration to even the most reluctant poet.

Hopkins, Lee Bennett. 2010. "Spring." In *Sharing the Seasons: A Book of Poems.* New York: Simon and Schuster.

A collection of twelve poems for each of the four seasons.

Klein, A. M. "Orders." 2000. In *Songs of Myself: An Anthology of Poems and Art*, ed. Georgia Heard. New York: Mondo.

The book matches poems and artwork and is a celebration of life.

***Companion pieces:***

Bedard, Michael. 1997. *The Divide.* New York: Bantam Doubleday Dell.

Burleigh, Robert. 2004. *Langston's Train Ride.* New York: Orchard.

MacLachlan, Patricia, and Emily MacLachlan. 2003. *Painting the Wind.* New York: HarperCollins.

McNaughton, Colin. 2001. *I'm Talking Big!* London: Walker Books.

A collection of poems and pictures by Colin McNaughton about all things big—dinosaurs, monsters, giants, etc., and other topics.

***Companion pieces:***

Hillman, Ben. 2007. *How Big Is It? A Big Book All About Bigness.* New York: Scholastic.

———. 2008. *How Fast Is It?* New York: Scholastic.

——— 2009. *How Weird Is It?* New York: Scholastic.

Palatini, Margie. 1999. *Moosetache.* New York: Hyperion.

———. 2000. *Mooseltoe.* New York: Hyperion.

Both books by Margie Palatini contain a scaffold found in the sample as part of the Your Turn Lesson.

Wolf, Allan. 2009. "Helping Hands." In *Falling Down the Page: A Book of List Poems*, ed. Georgia Heard. New York: Roaring Brook.

"Helping Hands" provides an easy scaffold for text innovations.

***Companion pieces:***

Ewald, Wendy. 2002. *The Best Part of Me: Children Talk About Their Bodies in Pictures and Words.* New York: Little, Brown.

Jenkins, Steve, and Robin Page. 2003. *What Do You Do with a Tail Like This?* Boston, MA: Houghton Mifflin.

Lorbiecki, Marybeth. 1998. *Sister Anne's Hands.* New York: Dial Books for Young Readers.

Martin, Jr., Bill, and John Archembault. 1998. *Here Are My Hands.* New York: Henry Holt.

Price, Hope Lynne. 1999. *These Hands.* New York: Hyperion.

Ryder, Joanne. 1994. *My Father's Hands.* New York: Morrow Junior.

## CHAPTER 4: ACROSTIC POETRY: ACCESSIBLE AND CHALLENGING

Aston, Dianna Hutts. 2011. *A Butterfly Is Patient.* San Francisco: Chronicle.

This book presents nonfiction in a poetic way accompanied by beautiful illustrations. Each big idea statement can be used as the basis for an acrostic poem.

Base, Graeme. 1996. *Animalia.* New York: Puffin.

This book is more than just a simple alphabet book. It is full of words and images that relate to each letter of the alphabet. When considered as a whole, it is an example of an abecedarian acrostic.

Harley, Avis. 2008. "Worldly Wise." In *The Monarch's Progress: Poems with Wings*. Honesdale, PA: Boyds Mills.

A collection of poems that capture the wonder of monarch butterflies. Although Harley uses several different poetic forms throughout, she chose the acrostic form to emphasize the four stages of metamorphosis. Additional facts about monarchs are also included.

***Companion pieces:***

Bunting, Eve. 1999. *Butterfly House.* New York: Scholastic.

Coville, Bruce. 2002. *The Prince of Butterflies.* New York: Harcourt.

Markle, Sandra. 2011. *Butterfly Tree.* Atlanta, GA: Peachtree.

————. 2009. "Sipping the Sunset." In *African Acrostics: A Word in Edgeways*. Somerville, MA: Candlewick.

A book of acrostics about African animals; contains examples of traditional acrostic poems, double acrostics (the first and last letters of each line), cross acrostics (read diagonally), and multiple acrostics (two types of poem in one); provides additional information on the acrostic forms and the animals used as subjects of the poems.

***Companion pieces:***

Aston, Dianna Hutts. 2006. *An Egg Is Quiet*. San Francisco, CA: Chronicle.

————. 2007. *A Seed Is Sleepy*. San Francisco, CA: Chronicle.

————. 2011. *A Butterfly Is Patient*. San Francisco, CA: Chronicle.

Hirschi, Ron. 1990. *Spring*. New York: Penguin.

A book rich in lyrical language to inspire poetry about spring.

Hummon, David. 1999. *Animal Acrostics*. Nevada City, CA: Dawn.

This book is a collection of acrostic poems about animals. Most of the poems are created with single words, but are read as connected ideas that convey the essence of the animal. Hummon uses punctuation to define and connect the thoughts.

Kitchen, Bert. 1988. *Animal Alphabet*. New York: Puffin.

A wordless book that features illustrations of each alphabet letter along with paintings of corresponding animals. On the last page of the book the animals depicted are identified in an abecedarian format.

Mowery, Will. "Acrostic." Used with permission of the author.

A poem that helps introduce the concept of acrostics.

————. "Recess." Used with permission of the author.

An acrostic poem that demonstrates voice and sharp focus.

Paolilli, Paul, and Dan Brewer. 2001. "Butterfly." In *Silver Seeds*. New York: Penguin Putnam.

The poets write acrostics as they follow the course of a day from dawn to dusk. Their acrostics link the lines together to form one thought or several connected thoughts about the topic of the poem which is also the poem's title.

***Companion pieces:***

Fletcher, Ralph. 1997. *Twilight Comes Twice*. New York: Clarion.

Hirschi, Ron. 1990. *Winter*. New York: Penguin.

Powell, Consie. 2003. *Amazing Apples*. Morton Grove, IL: Albert Whitman.
   Acrostic poems describe an apple orchard through the seasons. It is interesting to note that the dedication is written in the form of an acrostic poem. The book also includes a two-page spread that talks about the history of apples, what they are used for, the process of grafting, and suggestions for what you can do with apples.
   ***Companion piece:***
Gibbons, Gail. 1988. *The Seasons of Arnold's Apple Tree*. New York: Houghton Mifflin Harcourt.

Schnur, Steven. 1997. *Autumn: An Alphabet Acrostic*. New York: Clarion.
   Concise, direct, and accessible-to-all poetry.

———. 1999. *Spring: An Alphabet Acrostic*. New York: Clarion.
   Sights and smells of spring days and nights.

———. 2001. "Idle." In *Summer: An Alphabet Acrostic*. New York: Clarion.
   Poems that span early summer to late summer in content using appeal to the senses.

———. 2002. "Jewel." In *Winter: An Alphabet Acrostic*. New York: Clarion.
   This book captures the pleasure of the season with indoor and outdoor scenes. Schnur's books are all written as acrostic poems about the season.
   ***Companion pieces:***
Beach, Judi K. 2003. *Names for Snow*. New York: Hyperion.
Hirschi, Ron. 1990a. *Spring*. New York: Penguin.
———. 1990b. *Winter*. New York: Penguin.
Iverson, Diane. 1996. *Discover the Seasons*. Nevada City, CA: Dawn.

Young, Judy. 2005. "Drawing." In *R Is for Rhyme: A Poetry Alphabet*. Chelsea, MI: Sleeping Bear.
   A collection of poems that explains and illustrates various poetic tools, terms, and styles.

## CHAPTER 5: THE PERSONA POEM: WRITING IN THE VOICE OF ANOTHER

Fletcher, Ralph. 1997. "railroad tracks." In *Ordinary Things: Poems from a Walk in Early Spring*. New York: Simon & Schuster.
   Poems about the ordinary (or not so ordinary) things that Fletcher noticed on the walks he took while living in New Hampshire.

Florian, Douglas. 1999. "The Winter Tree." In *Winter Eyes*. New York: Greenwillow.
A collection of winter poems and paintings about winter using rhyme, celebrating the season and all that it entails.
**Companion piece:**
George, Kristine O'Connell. 1998. "Between Two Trees" and "Tree Traffic." In *Old Elm Speaks: Tree Poems*. New York: Clarion Books.

George, Kristine O'Connell. 1997. "Monkey Wrench." In *The Great Frog Race and Other Poems*. New York: Clarion.
This collection of poetry centers on observations of small things and an appreciation of nature. The author includes different types of poems such as haiku, concrete, and free verse.

Janeczko, Paul B., ed. 2001. *Dirty Laundry Pile: Poems in Different Voices*. New York: Harper-Collins.
A collection of persona poems in the voice of household objects and animals; a great source for teaching elements of style.

Janosco, Beatrice. 1966. "The Garden Hose." In *Reflections on a Gift of Watermelon Pickle . . . and Other Modern Verse*, ed. Stephen Dunning, Edward Leuders, and Hugh Smith. New York: Lothrop, Lee & Shepard.
The 114 poems found in this book were specifically chosen to appeal to young readers. Includes a wide range of works by well-known and also little-known poets. Other persona poems in this collection include "The Toaster," "Steam Shovel," and "The Bat."
**Companion piece:**
George, Kristine O'Connell. 1997. "Garden Hose." In *The Great Frog Race and Other Poems*. New York: Clarion.

Lewis, J. Patrick. 2005. "Empire State Building." In *Momumental Verses*. Washington, DC: National Geographic Society.
The poet celebrates timeless monuments around the world, often using the lines of the poem to create a shape that reflects the poem's subject. Several of the poems are written in the voice of the monument; includes additional information about each monument.
**Companion pieces:**
Hopkinson, Deborah. 2006. *Sky Boys: How They Built the Empire State Building*. New York: Random House.
Karas, G. Brian. 2002. *Atlantic*. New York: G. P. Putnam's Sons.
Siebert, Diane. 1992. *Mojave*. New York: HarperCollins.
———. 1996. *Sierra*. New York: HarperCollins.

MacLachlan, Patricia, and Emily MacLachlan Charest. 2010. *I Didn't Do It*. New York: HarperCollins.
Poems in the voice of young canines often using effective repetition, questions, and variation of print including size of type and use of boldface.

Mowery, Will. "A Slave to Grubby Hands." Used with permission of the author.
Persona poem written with humor.

Sidman, Joyce. 2006. "Letter to the Sun." In *Butterfly Eyes and Other Secrets of the Meadow*. Boston, MA: Houghton Mifflin.
This book combines poetry riddles and science. It takes us through a day in the meadow, beginning with the rising sun and ending with evening twilight.

————. 2007. *This Is Just to Say: Poems of Apology and Forgiveness*. Boston, MA: Houghton Mifflin.
A collection of apology poems written in different formats including haiku, two-part poems, and rhymes.
***Companion pieces:***
Bryant, Jen. 2008. *A River of Words: The Story of William Carlos Williams*. Grand Rapids, MI: Eerdmans Books for Young Readers.
Levine, Gail Carson. 2012. *Forgive Me, I Meant to Do It: False Apology Poems*. New York: HarperCollins.

————. 2010. *Dark Emperor and Other Poems of the Night*. New York: Houghton Mifflin Harcourt.
Poems (many personas) about night creatures with accompanying nonfiction selections.

Swinburne, Stephen. 2010. *Ocean Soup: Tide-Pool Poems*. Watertown, MA: Charlesbridge.
A collection of poems in the voices of tide-pool animals including a sea urchin, hermit crab, lobster, and sea slug; includes additional information on each of the animals.

Whipple, Laura. 2002. *If the Shoe Fits: Voices from Cinderella*. New York: Simon & Schuster.
Thirty-three poems written in the voices of the characters and objects from the Cinderella story, written for a sophisticated audience.

Winters, Kay. 2003. *Voices of Ancient Egypt*. Washington, DC: National Geographic.
A collection of poems written in the voices of people living in ancient Egypt and performing different jobs.

————. 2008. *Colonial Voices: Hear Them Speak*. New York: Dutton.
A collection of persona poems told from the viewpoints of people living during Colonial times.
***Companion piece:***
Schlitz, Laura Amy. 2007. *Good Masters! Sweet Ladies! Voices from a Medieval Village*. Cambridge, MA: Oxford Press.

# CHAPTER 6: POETRY FOR TWO VOICES

Bloome, Bruce. 2012. "Pet Preference." Used by permission of the author.
Filled with alliteration and written as two opposing opinions.
***Companion pieces:***
Baylor, Byrd. 1977. *Guess Who My Favorite Person Is*. New York: Charles Scribner's Sons.
————. 1995. *I'm In Charge of Celebrations*. New York: Simon & Schuster.
Kudlinski, Kathleen V. 2005. *The Sunset Switch*. Minnetonka, MN: NorthWord.
————. 2007. *The Seaside Switch*. Minnetonka, MN: NorthWord.

Fleischman, Paul. 1985. "Sparrows." In *I Am Phoenix: Poems for Two Voices*. New York: Harper-Collins.
A collection of poems about birds written for two voices.

————. 1988. "Honeybees." In *Joyful Noise: Poems for Two Voices*. New York: HarperCollins.
Poems for two voices that celebrate insects.

————. 2000. *Big Talk: Poems for Four Voices*. Cambridge, MA: Candlewick.
A collection of poems written for four voices; includes a "how to read this book" section and helpful hints for performance.

Franco, Betsy. 2009. "Backboard Rap." In *Messing Around on the Monkey Bars*. Somerville, MA: Candlewick.
A collection of nineteen poems written for two voices all about school related topics such as the bus, pencils, reports, recess, and homework.

Graves, Donald. 1996. "Explorers." In *Baseball, Snakes, and Summer Squash: Poems About Growing Up*. Honesdale, PA: Boyds Mills.
A wonderful story poem that could be written as a two-voice poem.

Harrison, David L. 2000. *Farmer's Garden: Rhymes for Two Voices.* Honesdale, PA: Boyds Mills.

This book is written as a series of rhymes for two voices. The farmer's dog wanders through the garden greeting all the creatures and plants he meets, resulting in friendly conversations.

Heard, Georgia. 1992. "Song of the Dolphin." In *Creatures of Earth, Sea, and Sky.* Honesdale, PA: Boyds Mills.

A persona poem with seesaw structures that will help students rewrite as a poem for two voices.

Hoberman, Mary Ann. 2001. "I Like." In *You Read to Me, I'll Read to You: Very Short Stories to Read Together.* New York: Little, Brown.

Poems written in two voices that are meant to be read by a child and an adult; the different parts are color-coded.

**Companion pieces:**

Hoberman, Mary Ann. 2004. *You Read to Me, I'll Read to You: Very Short Fairy Tales to Read Together.* New York: Little, Brown.

———. 2005. *You Read to Me, I'll Read to You: Very Short Mother Goose Tales to Read Together.* New York: Little, Brown.

———. 2007. *You Read to Me, I'll Read to You: Very Scary Tales to Read Together.* New York: Little, Brown.

———. 2010. *You Read to Me, I'll Read to You: Very Short Fables to Read Together.* New York: Little, Brown.

Holbrook, Sara. 2010. "Last Licks." In *Weird? (Me, Too!) Let's Be Friends.* Honesdale, PA: Boyds Mills.

A collection of poems that explore friendship; several are written for two or four voices; helpful suggestions for poetry writing are scattered throughout the book in the form of speech bubbles.

**Companion pieces:**

Brennan-Nelson, Denise. 2003. *My Momma Likes to Say.* Chelsea, MI: Sleeping Bear Press.

———. 2004. *My Teacher Likes to Say.* Chelsea, MI: Sleeping Bear Press.

———. 2007. *My Grandma Likes to Say.* Chelsea, MI: Sleeping Bear Press.

———. 2009. *My Daddy Likes to Say.* Chelsea, MI: Sleeping Bear Press.

Leedy, Loreen. 2003. *There's a Frog in My Throat: 440 Animal Sayings a Little Bird Told Me.* New York: Holiday House.

Mowery, Will. "the drip." Used by permission of the author.

    Accompanied by the poet's thoughts about his writing process for this poem.

Pappas, Theoni. 1991. "Triangles." In *Math Talk: Mathematical Ideas in Poems for Two Voices.*
San Carlos, CA: World Wide.

    A collection of poems written in two voices all about math concepts.

Wolf, Allan. 2009. "Helping Hands." In *Falling Down the Page: A Book of List Poems,* ed.
Georgia Heard. New York: Roaring Brook.

    This book is a collection of list poems. "Helping Hands" is a free-verse poem that we
fashioned into a poem for two voices.

    ***Companion pieces:***

    These picture books all have a seesaw (alternating) scaffold or clearly identified charac-
ters that can be read in two voices.

    Bauer, Caroline Feller. 1981. *My Mom Travels a Lot.* New York: Puffin.

    Charlip, Remy. 1964. *Fortunately.* New York: Simon and Schuster.

    Cuyler, Margery. 1991. *That's Good! That's Bad!* New York: Henry Holt.

    Fox, Mem. 1992. *Tough Boris.* New York: Harcourt Brace.

    James, Simon. 1991. *Dear Mr. Blueberry.* New York: Simon and Schuster.

    Orloff, Karen Kaufman. 2004. *I Wanna Iguana.* New York: G. P. Putnam's Sons.

    Viorst, Judith. 1990. *Earrings!* New York: Macmillan.

## ADDITIONAL POETRY BOOKS TOO GOOD TO MISS

Brenner, Barbara, ed. 1994. *The Earth Is Painted Green: A Garden of Poems About Our Planet.*
New York: Scholastic.

    A vast collection of poems from a variety of poets about nature; includes rhymed and
unrhymed verses, persona poems, and free verse.

Bulion, Leslie. 2011. *At the Sea Floor Café: Odd Ocean Critter Poems.* Atlanta, GA: Peachtree.

    A collection of poems about ocean creatures; includes additional information on the
poetic forms used (including a poem for two voices, haiku, and pantoum), a glossary of
scientific terms used, and informational passages on the sea creatures.

Carlson, Lori Marie, ed. 1998. *Sol a Sol: Bilingual Poems.* New York: Henry Holt.

    A collection of poems from various Hispanic American authors celebrating everyday
family activities; poems are written in English and Spanish.

Florian, Douglas. 2007. *Comets, Stars, the Moon, and Mars.* New York: Harcourt.
    Poems and paintings by Douglas Florian all about space-related objects.

Janeczko, Paul, ed. 2005. *A Kick in the Head: An Everyday Guide to Poetic Forms.* Cambridge,
    MA: Candlewick.
    This book is a collection of twenty-nine poems by different poets in different poetic
    forms; includes explanations of each poetic form.

———. 2009. *A Foot in the Mouth: Poems to Speak, Sing, and Shout.* Somerville, MA: Can-
    dlewick.
    A collection of poems by various poets meant to be read aloud; includes examples of
    poems for two voices, poems for three voices, list poems, bilingual poems, and others.

Lillegard, Dee. 2000. *Wake Up House! Rooms Full of Poems.* New York: Alfred A. Knopf.
    These poems describe common house objects in a fun and unique way, often personify-
    ing them; could be used as a study of punctuation and rhyme.

Loewen, Nancy. 2009. *Words, Wit, and Wonder: Writing Your Own Poem.* Minneapolis, MN:
    Picture Window.
    The text discusses twelve tools for writing great poems with examples for each tool as
    well as exercises for getting started, writers' tips, a glossary of terms, suggested readings,
    and an index for easy access.

Medina, Jane. 2004. *My Name Is Jorge: On Both Sides of the River.* Honesdale, PA: Boyds
    Mills.
    A collection of twenty-seven poems about the migrant experience told from the point of
    view of a child from Mexico.

Mora, Pat. 1985. *Chants.* Houston, TX: Arte Publico.
    Poems for older students centered on life in the Southwest's desert area; would appeal to
    Latino students.

Paul, Ann Whitford. 1999. *All by Herself.* New York: Browndeer.
    Fourteen famous women described in verse.

Salas, Laura Purdie. 2009. *Stampede! Poems to Celebrate the Wild Side of School.* New York:
    Clarion.
    A collection of eighteen poems with school as the setting; each poem compares student
    behavior to that of an animal. Filled with great ways to help students understand similes
    and metaphors; "Ducks in a Row" is a particularly good example of an acrostic poem.

Shapiro, Karen Jo. 2005. *Because I Could Not Stop My Bike and Other Poems*. Watertown, MA: Charlesbridge.
A collection of parodies of works by famous poets; best for upper elementary and middle school students.

Sidman, Joyce. 2002. *Eureka! Poems About Inventors*. Brookfield, CT: Millbrook.
A collection of sixteen poems about inventors throughout history who created useful things such as moveable type, Velcro, and the World Wide Web.

———. 2005. *Song of the Water Boatman and Other Pond Poems*. New York: Houghton Mifflin Harcourt.
A collection of poems about pond life written in a variety of formats; includes additional information about each creature or aspect of pond life.

———. 2008. *The World According to Dog: Poems and Teen Voices*. New York: Houghton Mifflin Harcourt.
A collection of poems by Sidman accompanied by short essays written by teens; includes black-and-white photos.

———. 2009. *Red Sings from Treetops: A Year in Colors*. New York: Houghton Mifflin Harcourt.
A celebration of color throughout the seasons and how colors change with the seasons; a picture book written in poetic form.

———. 2010a. *Dark Emperor and Other Poems of the Night*. New York: Houghton Mifflin Harcourt.
Poems (many personas) about night creatures with accompanying nonfiction selections.

———. 2010b. *Ubiquitous*. New York: Houghton Mifflin Harcourt.
Examples of a variety of poetry forms including persona, question, list, and diamante; includes an informational selection for each poem.

Siebert, Diane. 2006. *Tour America: A Journey Through Poems and Art*. San Francisco, CA: Chronicle.
Celebrates places and structures in the United States through poetry and mixed-media art.

Singer, Marilyn. 2011. *A Full Moon Is Rising*. New York: Lee & Low.
A collection of poems that takes us around the world to learn about beliefs, facts, customs, and celebrations about the full moon.

Spinelli, Eileen. 2004. *Feathers: Poems About Birds*. New York: Henry Holt.
A collection of poems all about birds. This book would serve as a wonderful companion piece for a unit on birds.

Thomas, Joyce Carol. 2008. *The Blacker the Berry*. New York: HarperCollins.
Poems celebrating the many shades of black.

Vecchione, Patrice, ed. 2002. *Whisper and Shout: Poems to Memorize*. Chicago: Cricket.
A collection of poems from a variety of poets including William Shakespeare, Emily Dickinson, Jack Prelutsky, and Nikki Giovanni; includes additional information on each of the poets.

Wilson, Edwin Graves, ed. 2007. *Maya Angelou*. New York: Sterling.
A collection of poems by Maya Angelou that is part of the Poetry for Young People series; includes a brief introduction to each of Angelou's poems; a user-friendly format with vocabulary defined at the bottom of each page.

Worth, Valerie. 2007. *Animal Poems*. New York: Farrar, Straus and Giroux.
Written in free verse; accompanying cut paper illustrations by Steve Jenkins bring animals to life.

Yolen, Jane. 2005. *Snow, Snow: Winter Poems for Children*. Honesdale, PA: Boyds Mills.
Thirteen poems about winter accompanied by striking photographs.

———. 2007. *Shape Me a Rhyme*. Honesdale, PA: Boyds Mills.
Twelve elegant poems about shapes found in nature; connections to math and art (symmetry and shapes) can be made.

———. 2009. *An Egret's Day*. Honesdale, PA: Boyds Mills Press.
Poems and photos about the daily life of the Great Egret.

Yolen, Jane, and Heidi E. Y. Stemple. *Dear Mother, Dear Daughter: Poems for Young People*. Honesdale, PA: Boyds Mills.
Seventeen pairs of sensitive verse written by a real-life mother and daughter (Yolen and Stemple), offering thoughts on adolescent issues.

# Afterword

Poems provide a unique vehicle for reading, writing, and thinking. They can easily be tucked into the work we do across the day because they are fairly short. They help us make connections with the characters, places, and events in the literature we are reading. They help us think and write about the events and feelings we share with our family and friends. They provide a way for us to express our thinking about the people and places we study across the curriculum and learn about in the media.

Poems are a wonderful way to fill in missing background knowledge that students need in order to accommodate new learning. The potential for vocabulary growth is tremendous; poets are the masters of the English language and use words in precise and unfamiliar contexts.

We hope the thinking and the poems we have provided throughout this book will help you use poetry in meaningful ways in your reading and writing classrooms. We tried to provide a menu of choices so that the poems can be used across grade levels to help target the needs of the students in your class. Recently, Rose began working in classrooms and with small groups of students in kindergarten through grade five. She used some of the poems successfully with students from a variety of grade levels, choosing the focus of the lesson to match the needs of the group. For example, with second graders who were still establishing decoding strategies, she used "The Winter Tree" by Douglas Florian, which focuses on sound patterns associated with the long "e" sound. She used this same poem with another Florian poem, "Winter Burrows," with a group of fourth graders to teach comparing and contrasting.

We hope this practical book will move you beyond more traditional teaching approaches and allow you to explore some innovative practices using poetry to make connections among concrete observations and the infinite possibilities of our imaginations.

Our friend and colleague Bruce Bloome, a fourth-grade teacher at Upper Moreland Intermediate School and a poet in his own right, shared his thinking about the power of poetry with us:

Come and share the words with me,
share your thoughts and dreams through poetry,
dare to see beyond what you can see,
through the skillfully-crafted words.

A poem is more than endless rhymes.
It's a pathway through our hardest times.
Through words our spirits climb and climb,
and we find our way back home.

A poem can be a way to share.
Two voices can go anywhere.
Their words entwined will take you there,
in harmonious harmony.

A poem can paint you in and out,
a portrait of what you're about,
It can scream for you when you can't shout.
and send your message to the world.

A poem can grow from just one word,
a phrase, a quip that you have heard,
it will sprout and blossom, word by word,
into a bountiful word bouquet.

A poem can be a list of things,
connected thoughts like golden rings,
like birds on a wire, the lyrics sing,
and your thoughts will shape and soar.

A poem inspires us all to write.
It gives us wings, our thoughts take flight,
our emotions soaring like a kite,
with our heads among the clouds.

Come and share your words with me.
The written word can set you free.
A poet everyone can be,
just spread your wings and try.

# References

Allen, Janet. 1999. *Words, Words, Words: Teaching Vocabulary in Grades 4–12*. Portland, ME: Stenhouse.

Bransford, John D., Brown, Ann L., and Cocking, Rodney R., eds. 2001. *How People Learn: Brain, Mind, Experience, and School*. Washington, DC: National Research Council.

Bromley, Karen D'Angelo. 1996. *Webbing with Literature: Creating Story Maps with Children's Books*. Needham Heights, MA: Allyn and Bacon.

Carey, Michael A. 1989. *Poetry: Starting from Scratch*. Lincoln, NE: Foundation.

Fletcher, Ralph. 1996. *A Writer's Notebook: Unlocking the Writer Within You*. New York: Avon.

———. 2002. *Poetry Matters: Writing a Poem from the Inside Out*. New York: Harper-Collins.

Flynn, Nick, and Shirley McPhillips. 2000. *A Note Slipped Under the Door: Teaching from Poems We Love*. Portland, ME: Stenhouse.

Glover, Mary Kenner. 1999. *A Garden of Poets: Poetry Writing in the Elementary Classroom.* Urbana, IL: NCTE.

Graham, Paula W., ed. 1999. *Speaking of Journals: Children's Book Writers Talk About Their Diaries, Notebooks, and Sketchbooks.* Honesdale, PA: Boyds Mills.

Graves, Donald H. 1994. *A Fresh Look at Writing.* Portsmouth, NH: Heinemann.

Heard, Georgia. 1989. *For the Good of the Earth and Sun: Teaching Poetry.* Portsmouth, NH: Heinemann.

Holbrook, Sara. 2005. *Practical Poetry: A Nonstandard Approach to Meeting Content-Area Standards.* Portsmouth, NH: Heinemann.

Hopkins, Lee Bennett. 1987. *Pass the Poetry, Please!* New York: Harper and Row.

Israel, Susan E., with Michelle M. Israel, eds. 2006. *Poetic Possibilities: Using Poetry to Enhance Literacy Learning.* Newark, DE: International Reading Association.

Janeczko, Paul B., ed. 1994. *Poetry from A to Z: A Guide for Young Writers.* New York: Macmillan.

———. 1999. *How to Write Poetry.* New York: Scholastic.

———. 2005. *A Kick in the Head: An Everyday Guide to Poetic Forms.* Cambridge, MA: Candlewick.

Laminack, Lester L., and Reba Wadsworth. 2006. *Learning Under the Influence of Language and Literature: Making the Most of Read-Alouds Across the Day.* Portsmouth, NH: Heinemann.

Loewen, Nancy. 2009. *Words, Wit, and Wonder: Writing Your Own Poem.* Minneapolis, MN: Picture Window.

McLaughlin, Maureen, and Mary Beth Allen. 2002. *Guided Comprehension: A Teaching Model for Grades 3–8.* Newark, DE: International Reading Association.

McPhillips, Shirley. 2012. "Coming into a World of Poetry." *The Stenhouse Blog.* http://blog.stenhouse.com/archives/2012/04/02/coming-into-a-world-of-poetry/.

Miller, Debbie. 2002. *Reading with Meaning: Teaching Comprehension in the Primary Grades.* Portland, ME: Stenhouse.

Padgett, Ron, ed. 1987. *The Teachers and Writers Handbook of Poetic Forms.* New York: Teachers and Writers Collaborative.

Portalupi, JoAnn, and Ralph Fletcher. 2001. *Nonfiction Craft Lessons: Teaching Informational Writing K–8.* Portland, ME: Stenhouse.

Prelutsky, Jack. 2008. *Pizza, Pigs, and Poetry: How to Write a Poem.* New York: Greenwillow Books.

Routman, Regie. 2000. *Conversations: Strategies for Teaching, Learning, and Evaluating* Portsmouth, NH: Heinemann.

# Index

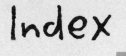

## Z

## Y